Simple Wonders

A Book of Reflections

CHRISTOPHER DE VINCK

CHARIS
SERVANT PUBLICATIONS
ANN ARBOR, MICHIGAN

Charis Books is an imprint of Servant Publications especially designed to serve Roman Catholics.

```
Servant Publications—Mission Statement
We are dedicated to publishing books that spread the gospel of Jesus Christ,
help Christians to live in accordance with that gospel, promote renewal in the
church, and bear witness to Christian unity.
```

Previous hardcover edition published by Zondervan Publishing House, ISBN: 0-310-20406-2.

This updated paperback edition published by
Servant Publications
P.O. Box 8617
Ann Arbor, Michigan 48107
www.servantpub.com

Cover design: Steve Eames, Ann Arbor, Michigan

03 04 05 06 10 9 8 7 6 5 4 3 2 1

Printed in the United States of America
ISBN 1-56955-381-5

Contents

Stop and consider God's wonders.
Job 37:14

Introduction

On February 1, 1960, Pope John XXIII was quoted as saying, "It often happens that I wake at night and begin to think about a serious problem and decide I must tell the pope about it. Then I wake up completely and remember that I am the pope!" John was called the popular pope, the people's pope, because of his wit and humility.

We live in a world that thrives on prestige, money, power. When we return to our childlike qualities, the ways of the "important" world do not seem so important after all.

I was dazzled when I received a phone call many years ago from the Vatican. "Dr. de Vinck, we are calling to see if you are still alive." The cardinal's office wanted to know. Yes, yes I was still alive.

The ambassador to the Vatican from Venezuela read one of my books a long time ago about my disabled brother, and because the Vatican was sponsoring an international conference on disabled people and the church, I was asked to give the closing presentation at the convocation. "You will stay in the Vatican. We will fly you from New York. We want you to meet Pope John Paul. We will mail you information."

When I thanked the man, I hung up the phone and walked into the living room where Roe, my wife, was sitting on the couch reading. I had news.

"Roe," I said with the voice of a king. "I've been invited to speak at the Vatican."

Roe looked up from her book and said, "That's very nice."

I tried again, nearly with a flourish of my hand. "They want me to give the closing speech at one of their international conferences."

Roe looked up from her book, said that she was very pleased, and returned to her book.

I tried one last time. "And they want me to meet the pope." That would impress her.

"He seems like a good man."

Roe keeps me grounded, but I was ready, just the same, to take on the Vatican, Rome, the Holy Father and dazzle them and be dazzled.

I was flown to Rome, driven to the Vatican, given a special pass to enter Vatican City at will. I was given a tour of St. Peter's Basilica. I was given a tour of the Roman ruins. I saw the work of Michaelangelo. I shook the hand of Pope John Paul as he whispered, "God bless you Christopher." But what delighted me the most was the coconut seller.

As I walked with my tour guide along the streets of Rome, we came upon a man dressed simply as he stood beside this contraption. It was a layer of five, clear glass shelves layered on top of each other with about six inches between them. In the middle of the shelves was a clear tube that ended on the top of the first shelf, and water was bubbling out of the tip of the tube. This water spread across the face of the top shelf, then dribbled down to the next shelf, and the water on the next shelf spread across the smooth surface and dribbled down to the next shelf. There was a constant flow of water gurgling from the tub and flowing from shelf to shelf, and on each shelf were thinly sliced pieces of white coconut. I thought this was such a clever way to keep the pieces of coconut cool. This was better than Willy Wonka's Chocolate Factory or Jules Verne's time machine.

When I returned home from my trip, Roe asked me about the Vatican. It was big, but there was this coconut seller.

She asked me about the pope. He was very nice, but the coconut seller had this row of shelves.

Roe asked me about my talk. "Oh, there were many people, and the slices of coconut were kept cool by the water that dribbled down from shelf to shelf."

Henri Nouwen asked, when he invited me to visit him at Harvard, "How do you do that?" How do I write, he wanted to know. Henri and I had many conversations about writers, poetry, the cadence of the sentence, the use of details, and I said to him often, just tell a simple story, focus on the simple, everyday occurrences. People want to know that they can find wisdom and solace right in their own neighborhood, right in their own experiences.

All religion can be condensed in one simple phrase: love one another. All history can be defined in two words: evil and holiness. All cultivation can be defined in a single word: seed. We have extraordinary explanations concerning the beginning of the universe, when it is enough to say that matter was infused with a purpose. When the excitable newscasters state with tones of urgency about the impending winter storm warning, I look outside and look at the snow shovel and the narrow driveway.

The writer's task, I believe, is to take the extraordinary and reveal it as ordinary, and to take the ordinary, the simple, the small, and reveal it as extraordinary.

When I was a high school student, my teachers of English tried to explain the meaning and value of poetry. No matter what poem we read in class, I always had the same complaint: "If Robert Frost wants to say something about fences, why doesn't he just come right out and say it instead of talking about neighbors and good relationships?"

As I look back, much of what it meant to be young seemed to depend upon mystery and on the unavoidable circumstance of being ignorant. I just did not see things the way that older people did. I would look at a painting and see a horse with some old guy leaning against a lance. I would listen to a classical piece of music and hear just a bunch of toots and violins.

Youth skates on the surface of the ice; but then, as we grow older, a bell rings, or a word is said, or a particular color is illuminated, and slowly there is the realization that there is something more.

I remember kneeling one winter when I was a boy on the ice of the swamp beyond the woods of my house. My sister zoomed ahead of me. Johnny, my neighbor and best friend, chased after Anne. I leaned over the ice and began swirling my glove on the ice's surface. At first I saw a faint orange color, and then I saw a goldfish looking up at me through the ice.

"Hey, you guys! There's a fish under here!"

"What did you expect to see?" Johnny said with laughter. "An elephant?"

I never thought about fish in winter. Something was down there, under the surface, still swimming around.

When I read for the first time John Steinbeck's novel *The Grapes of Wrath*, I saw and felt things that I had never seen or felt before. The people in that book were in great pain, and I suffered with them. I never felt those things before about a book.

I knew that I wanted to be a writer when I read the poetry of William Carlos Williams. He wrote about old men, young men, old women, and young women. He sang about trees and grass and children with twirling toys. He was able to write about a funeral, about a woman giving birth, about a man dancing in a room, in ways that made me understand things under the surface of the ice. Williams taught me how to write in the language of an ordinary person saying ordinary things. The writer's magic, however, is in the ability to identify the ordinary in the name of beauty, or passion, or loneliness, or God.

This book is a collection of ordinary moments in a single life written in the name of beauty, passion, loneliness, and in the name of God. It is my hope that this book helps you define the simple wonders that surround you each day. I would like you to stop skating for a second and kneel down beside me. Here, like this. Now, take your glove and swirl it on the ice. Careful. Look down through the ice and take a good look. See the fish?

Under the surface, the fish are swimming.

Pope John Paul XXIII must have smiled when he said, "The feeling of my smallness and my nothingness always kept me good company." It is the feeling of our smallness that sometimes discourages us, and yet we, each one of us, are the grand purpose of existence.

We are the simple wonders making our way as best we can chewing on cool slices of fresh coconuts.

God in Surprising Places

Surely the Lord is in this place, and I was not aware of it.

I met an old woman in a nursing home many years ago when I was in high school. My class was supposed to write a paper on someone over seventy. I didn't know anyone over seventy except for my grandparents, but they were living in Belgium. Then I thought of the idea: I'll visit a nursing home and ask permission if I could meet someone for my English assignment.

When I entered the brick building I walked up to the front desk. A kind woman with glasses sent me to the director's office.

After I explained my assignment to the director, she sent me to room six.

Room six had a bed, a single chair, a desk, and a single picture of a rose on the wall. Sitting in the chair was Mrs. Murphy. She was bent over knitting diligently. Her needles clicked and ticked. When I knocked on her door Mrs. Murphy looked up from her knitting and squinted.

"Yes?" she asked.

"I'm from the high school. I'm supposed to write an essay about someone over seventy."

"Step out of the hall light. Come in. Come in." Mrs. Murphy stopped knitting and patted the bed beside her. "Sit here."

I slowly entered the room which smelled like lemon candy. I sat on the left back corner of the little bed.

Mrs. Murphy returned to her knitting.

"What are you making?" I asked.

"God's in my basket," she answered.

Because I thought that she wasn't very good at hearing, I spoke a bit louder.

"What's in your basket, Mrs. Murphy?"

She stopped knitting again, turned her face in my direction, smiled and repeated "God's in my basket."

I looked around the room and finally noticed her knitting basket at the foot of her chair. It was filled with various balls of wool. I leaned forward a little to get a small peek just in case I might catch a glimpse of God.

"Oh, He's there." Mrs. Murphy smiled.

"How can you tell?" I asked.

"I've prayed for Him to come, and He has." With that, Mrs. Murphy returned to her basket and didn't say a word after that. No matter what I asked, she just continued rocking, smiling, and rocking some more.

Finally I stood up, thanked the old woman, and walked back into the bright hall light. Just before I left the building, the director stepped out from another room. She smiled and asked me how things went.

"Not so well," I said with a disappointed edge to my voice. After all, my writing project was a failure. "She thinks that God is in her knitting basket."

"What is your name?" the woman asked.

"Christopher."

"That means *Christ bearer*, doesn't it?" she asked, more as a statement of fact than a question to be verified. "What did you think of Mrs. Murphy?"

"I think she is a little crazy."

"She was when she first arrived," the director said. "When her husband died, she was alone. They didn't have any children. She has no family. She is ninety-three. All she wanted to do was die. That was five years ago. Then she said that all she wanted was peace. I suggested that she pray for peace. So that is what she did. A few months later she discovered knitting. A woman who came to us for a recreation hour taught Mrs. Murphy how to knit. In six months she was knitting everyone socks. At the Christmas fair she sold over a thousand dollars worth of socks, wool dolls, sweaters, blankets. She taught knitting in the local grade school as a volunteer. The children from the school would invite her home for dinner at least three times a week. Mrs. Murphy was the most popular person in our neighborhood, and in our nursing home. She was truly happy."

"But what about now?" I asked.

"Well, she no longer remembers very much. She has become so old and sick. She has forgotten everyone's name."

"But she can still knit," I said.

"Yes, Christopher, she can still knit, and she is at peace. And something else, too. She says only one sentence."

"God's in her basket."

"Yes, the God of peace."

I never did write my essay for school, but two weeks later a brown package waited for me when I returned home. Inside I found a beautiful, wool brown sweater, just my size. I also found a note in a small, white envelope:

Dear Christopher:

Mrs. Murphy asked that we send you this gift. She thought you'd like a bit of God to keep you warm.

Mrs. Murphy died three days ago. She was very happy. Stop by and visit us again someday.

Sincerely,
Sister Claire Roberts, OFM

How often do you take an active role in seeking out the existence of God? How often do you look around for proof that Christ lived and died for our salvation? Do you ever doubt that God is always beside you? Have no fear. He, our God of peace and mercy, is tugging at your sleeve with his unconditional love.

Lord of the day, keeper of divine secrets, help me see your face in the face of those I meet today. Help me recognize your work in all that I see. I look for your guidance. I am blessed with the ability to do your will. In the name of you, Father, I pray for renewed vision so that I may clearly see my way to your home of peace, to your house of eternity. In the name of you, Father, I pray.

Touch of God

Father, into your hands I commit my spirit.

LUKE 23:46

*D*uring my visit to a second grade classroom in the school district where I work, I asked children what they do when they are sad. Some said that they walk up to their room and rest on their beds and think. A boy said that he reads. A girl said that she likes to color when she is sad. Then a boy to my right, sitting in the circle, said, "Well, I pretend that I'm sick."

I didn't understand, so I asked the boy why he did this.

"Well, when I'm sad, I need someone, so I pretend that I am sick. Someone will feel my forehead. I like it when my mother puts her hand on my forehead."

I have been thinking about this answer. A minister friend of mine said that when he visits the hospital, it seems that the best thing he can do is to place his hand on someone's forehead. "People smile almost every time I do this, no matter how ill the person might be."

We live in an age where pills, heating pads, and exercise machines seem to help make us feel better.

Is the hand of another person the hand of healing? When my two sons and my daughter were born, I wanted to kiss the hands of the doctor, the first human hands to hold my children. A farmer runs his hands through the spring soil. A woman combs her hair with her extended fingers.

Often, in the great Russian icons, the image of Christ is holding up his right hand in a blessing. All in the universe stands before the raised hand of God. Perhaps the warm sun upon our bodies is the hand of a healing God.

When I am sad I often return to my desk and I begin to write. The words seem to speak; the words seem to form an image of a person speaking. Often it is my father waving to me across the distance of my own adulthood; often it is the image of my mother. I remember how my mother held a stone on the flat of her palm. She liked to display simple things. "Look at this beautiful stone," she said. What was beautiful was my mother's hand in the air, stretched out before me.

A few nights ago my daughter Karen had a fever. I placed my hand on her forehead, and she smiled. "Your hand feels so cool. Please leave it there."

God reaches down to us with his hands to soothe our pain. We can feel the power of this healing though the embrace of a neighbor, a doctor, or a loved one. We can sense his touch against our cheeks when we walk out of the house in the morning air. How difficult it is sometimes to offer back to God a human touch upon the face of his infinite glory.

God of all people, I give thanks for the cradle of your hands. Rock me back and forth today between the moon and sun, protect me today with a single touch of your fingertip. Trace on my forehead a small cross when I need your grace. I give thanks to you my God for your touching my life, for being my life. For this I give thanks.

Delighting in God's Creation

In the beginning God created the heavens and the earth.

Genesis 1:1

*W*e are funny human beings. We take too much for granted. If we never saw a tree and we suddenly stepped around a corner and saw, for the first time, an oak tree, we would think it was the most extraordinary thing that ever existed.

If we never saw a jet passenger plane, and suddenly a Boeing 747 flew overhead, we would think, perhaps, a thunder god zoomed by.

If we never saw a fish, a cat, a car, a strawberry before, how wondrous these things would appear. Unfortunately the more we are exposed to something, the more and more of a distance we create between the true marvel and the stale attitude.

People who create a circus try to battle this flaw of ours. They arrange animals in a way that force us to stop and look closely. An elephant is, well, just an elephant, but make ten elephants march around a circle, or stand on each other's backs, then you have something extraordinary. But can you think of a more extraordinary creature than the elephant. (This is even a wonderful word: *elephant*.)

Shoot a person out of a cannon, and we look closely at a human being. The circus dazzles us with tigers pawing at the trainer, seals climbing ladders, bears dancing. What is left if we take the music away, and the ringmaster, and the clowns, and the costumes?

What is left if we wash the paint off the elephant's hide? What if we take the hat off the bear's head? What is left? Just a bear; just a few elephants and men and women standing around on the saw-dust.

If we can teach ourselves to look closely at the things that surround us, we would be dazzled. A dog, a *DOG* is an extraordinary creature. Did you ever appreciate a screen in the window? What a wonderful invention. I think a bicycle is one of the most extraordinary inventions, all that spinning and chains and balance and metal. We can travel faster on a bicycle than a running athlete, and visit anywhere in town without gasoline, money, insurance, or a license.

Do you remember the delight you felt after you created something: a flower arrangement, a painting, a garden, a baby, a report, a song? Can you imagine the delight God must have felt after he created the sun, the moon, the earth, and all its treasures? Can you imagine how pleased he was when he created *you?*

God the artist. God the craftsman. God the maker. Walk though the day as if you are visiting an art gallery and take delight in all that you see framed in heaven's gold.

I think God must have had lots of fun when he created carrots.

I am worthy, Lord, of a place beside the redwood trees. I am worthy to stand in the lilies of the field. I am worthy, Lord, to swim with the dolphins, to breathe the mountain air. I am worthy this day to take my place in your creation. I am worthy, Lord, of your delight, Master, Carpenter, Builder of stars and hope. I am worthy.

The Kindness of God

But when the kindness and love of God our Savior appeared.

TITUS 3:4

*J*osh was the old man next door. He raised his own chickens, sold eggs, planted his own garden, and sold vegetables. I was afraid of Josh when I was a child. He was always stooped over when he walked. He could not speak many words in English. I once saw him chop the head off one of his chickens. Josh didn't have many teeth.

One early September morning my mother asked me if I would run down to Josh and buy some tomatoes. My mother wanted to add some flavor to her stew. I never walked to Josh's house alone before. I always accompanied my older brother or sister whenever we were asked to make a purchase down at Josh's place.

Always an obedient boy, I did as my mother asked after she handed me a dollar. After I stood before Josh's house for a long time, I pulled the string of the bell that hung from the front door.

"Yes?" he asked as he opened the door and looked at me.

"My mother would like two tomatoes." I wanted to run.

"In the back." Josh closed the door, and by the time I stepped to the back of his house, he was already there standing beside his vegetable stand. I watched as he reached over with his big hands and lifted four tomatoes and placed them into a brown bag. He reached down and handed me the bag. "No charge." I looked up at him and he smiled, revealing his few teeth and his good heart.

I never forgot Josh over these thirty years. A little kindness goes a long way.

Sometimes we think that God is a frightening power that oversees all that we do with a gruff cast of his eye. Like a child confronting the strong, old vegetable man, we can sometimes be intimidated by the truth and mystery in God's love for us, but then his infinite kindness is revealed in a minister's words, in an embrace from a parent, in a quiet understanding that our suffering no longer exists.

You are placed in many positions of power: in your home, in your work, in your relationships with strangers. Such power exercised with kindness not only will earn you great respect, but will also allow others to see you smile, a human, God-given trait we sometimes forget to exhibit. Perhaps you can extend a kind gesture toward the first person you see today.

I can stand before you, Lord, in meekness, in my fear of you and tremble, but in your kindness you have said "Do not be afraid, for I am with you" (Gn 26:24). In your kindness I sing. In your kindness I take comfort. In you, God, I am not afraid.

God's Smile

Do not pay attention to every word people say.

ECCLESIASTES 7:21

It is unusual these days to see a man wearing a straw hat. It is unusual to see a man wearing a hat at all.

Often when I am driving through my little town in northern New Jersey I see this man with white hair winding his way through the streets wearing a simple straw hat on his head. I often see him carrying a newspaper under his arm as he walks.

One afternoon while I was standing in line at the bank, the man with the straw hat entered and stood in line behind me.

I turned around and said, "I've always admired your hat."

"What?" he asked.

"Your hat. I often notice you walking in town with your straw hat."

"What's the matter with my hat?" he asked in a cross voice.

"I just don't see many straw hats."

"Why not?"

"I think your hat looks nice, something old-fashioned."

"What about old? Did you say I'm old?"

I wasn't sure if I should have continued with my failing attempt at expressing my delight in seeing this man and his hat, so I tried to change the subject. "Nice weather."

"It's supposed to rain. My wife said to take my hat. It's made in Panama." He pulled the hat from his head, turned it upside down and pointed to the label.

"It's a beautiful hat," I said.

"I hate it, but my wife makes me wear it, so I wear it to make her happy." Then the man with a straw hat offered for the first time a genuine smile.

It is difficult to see God in a grumpy old man, until that man smiles and suddenly, there is the light, the changed person, the true person revealed, the child of God.

Someone said to me once that we can see the features of God in a single smile. Look for that smile in the people you meet.

Now each time I drive by the man in the straw hat, I beep my horn. He turns, tips his hat in a quick gesture, smiles, and waves hello.

God of my smiles, remind me to laugh when I am happy; remind me to express joy when I am satisfied. Remind me, God, to rest in my happiness when I have done your will. Keep me in your heart that is laughing.

Inside Goodness

Therefore, if your whole body is full of light, and no part of it dark, it will be completely lighted, as when the light of a lamp shines on you.
LUKE 11:36

We were out, my family and I, selecting the best pumpkin we could find for our front steps. "This one," Karen decided. "It looks like the carriage in Cinderella."

As I carried the pumpkin to the car, Karen, who was six at the time, and her two brothers (ages four and eight) ran ahead of Roe and me. Autumn belongs to children dancing before their parents upon the brown fields of a new season.

"Can we carve the pumpkin?" David called out from the backseat of the car as we drove home.

"Can I help?" Michael asked.

"What can I do?" Karen wondered aloud.

"You can give the pumpkin his heart," I said.

"Yuck," was Karen's response.

After we pulled into the driveway, I lifted the pumpkin to my right shoulder as the children followed behind me into the house.

Roe spread a section of the *New York Times* on the kitchen table. David carried a knife over from the drawer. Michael asked if we could roast the seeds. "We did that in school." Karen was silent.

After I cut the wide cap from the pumpkin we each took turns pulling the seeds, string, and goo out of the pumpkin's middle. Michael liked the goo. Then I began carving a face: two triangles for eyes, one triangle for the nose, and a crooked, nearly toothless smile.

Karen began to cry. "What about me?" She didn't like the goo or the seeds.

"Open the bottom drawer, Karen, and bring me the pumpkin's heart."

She stepped up to the drawer. "There's nothing here but a bunch of old candles."

"Yes," I said. "Please bring me one, Karen."

She brought me a white candle that I lit and placed deep into the belly of the pumpkin. Roe turned out the kitchen light. The children laughed as the dim candle reflected against their small faces.

"The pumpkin's heart," Karen whispered.

Yes, the pumpkin's heart, I thought as I sat beside Roe and the children.

What glows from the inside often reflects what is on the outside. Have you allowed the inside goodness of you to shine recently?

Do you sometimes keep yourself hidden from those you love? Are you afraid to reveal yourself sometimes out of fear or embarrassment? Those around you will notice the shadow and discomfort on your face.

Trust in God's love for you. Allow his light to illuminate your whole body for when the eyes of those around you are focused on God's creation, your light will not be pushed aside by the shade. God's light will lead you to security and into the valley of the sun.

Carve a pumpkin this autumn. I am sure there is a heart to be lit somewhere in your house.

God of the sun, God of the stars, teach me how to collect the warmth of your light that shines against my heart. Protect me from the shadow of evil. Protect me with the sword of your light. Cut away the darkness. Today I am open for the radiance of your power.

Are There Turtles in Heaven?

Faith is being sure of what we hope for and certain of what we do not see.

HEBREWS 11:1

*D*o you remember a time in your childhood when you questioned the existence of heaven?

I remember when I was a boy I was walking through the swamps behind our house along the bank of a narrow, deep canal. Suddenly the still water began to undulate; small waves rippled against the bank. I leaned over and looked into the water. I saw the faint outline of a huge snapping turtle pass before me, then it dove deep into the dark water and disappeared. Where do turtles go, I wondered.

"Are there turtles in heaven?" I asked my mother later that day.

"Of course there are. Lots of them."

As I grew older I continued to ask about the quality of heaven.

"Can I bring my cat Moses there?"

"Yes."

"Will I recognize you, Mom?"

"Yes."

"Can we have raspberries in heaven? I like raspberries."

"Yes."

In my early twenties I asked, "With all that we know about science, is heaven perhaps just beyond the expanding universe?"

And now that I am in my forties I have been asking myself a more direct question: "Is there a heaven?" I find myself asking this question more and more because I do not want to leave my wife and children when I someday die. I do not want them to be alone. I want to be with them always.

So this is what I have come to believe: heaven is a place for cats and turtles, and for my mother and father, and for my wife and children, and for everyone.

My life is connected to an acceptance that some questions can only be answered with one word: faith.

Christ promised us paradise as he was dying on the cross. I believe in that promise. I believe in life everlasting. I believe in God the Father almighty, the Creator of heaven and earth, in all things seen and unseen. I believe. I believe.

Do you?

When I am cold, you provide me with warmth. When I am lonely you sit beside me and we talk. When I am old you tell me not to be afraid. Thank you God for these examples of your mercy and generosity. When I fear death, you remind me of salvation. I pray to you dear God and give thanks for your promise that I will someday join you in heaven.

Breaking Through the Clouds

The sun rises and the sun sets, and hurries back to where it rises.

ECCLESIASTES 1:5

I was reminded of a simple truth while flying home from a recent talk I delivered in Toronto.

I arrived at the airport a bit early, so I sat and read the newspaper about all the gloom and sadness. The gray sky outside was beginning to grow darker. Storm clouds were forming.

After we were allowed to settle inside the plane, after the jet zoomed off heading south, I felt a bit lonely, caught between leaving my new friends and not yet being home with my wife and children.

Something happened. As the Air Canada jet climbed and climbed, I looked out the window into the dark, gray fog that draped itself on the entire country; then suddenly, the plane broke through the clouds and we were flying under a blue, clean sky with the bronze sun setting in the west.

We can wonder at the meaning of gloomy, rainy days, but we forget that we need the rain to keep the soil rich for our food. God built this house, this universe for us.

No matter how gloomy the day appears, no matter how much fog, rain, or snow makes you feel depressed, remember that God is always there behind the curtain polishing the brass sun.

Today look at one of your troubles and try to see clearly through the fog to that bright, bronze-colored solution.

Open to me, oh Lord, a glimpse of your light. How easily I fall into darkness. How easily I feel the cold. Grant me your vision, Lord. Let me see beyond what appears as fog, and gloom, and rain. Let me sing to the hidden way. Let me dance toward the dawn's resurrection.

Safe Haven

When you enter a house, first say, "Peace to this house."

LUKE 10:5

I was sitting on the couch reading a wonderful book, *Iron and Silk* by Mark Saltzman. The book is about Mr. Saltzman's two years he spent as an English teacher in China. He is a writer with a clear eye for description and a strong heart full of humor and wisdom.

I was reading the section where some Chinese children were frightened by a ghost story Mark was retelling when I felt a pressure on my legs, then a full weight of someone crawling up on my chest.

Michael, my young son, had come inside the house after a ride on his bicycle. Without a word he simply wiggled onto my lap and curled into a comfortable position.

It pleases me greatly that our children feel comfortable enough with my wife and me to simply plop themselves down upon us whenever they feel the need to do so.

It takes a little more ribcage strength when David, our older son, needs a father or mother pillow.

We all need a safe haven of trust and love to return to after a difficult day at work, or after a tough ride around the neighborhood.

Before Christ was arrested and crucified, he walked to the Mount of Olives. In his fear of the upcoming events, he asked his Father, God almighty, "If you are willing, take this cup from me"

(Lk 22:42). Jesus, too, needed a safe haven. Where did he go for protection? It was not a physical place. It was not Mount Olive. In his need for safety Jesus returned to God his Father, and then he prayed.

Our true haven is in our prayers to God. We petition the Lord for guidance, for help, for comfort. He is there to do these things. He has promised this to us.

We are reminded each day that God provides his protection for us, just as he sent his confidence and love down to his Son, Jesus Christ.

"Why are you sleeping?" the Lord asked his disciples. "Get up and pray so that you will not fall into temptation." I stand up and pray to the Holy One. I stand up and pray. I am not a person of a lonely distance from you, God my protector. You are here beside me. Hear my whisper. Hear my prayer. Amen, amen I say to you with gratitude for your comfort.

The Sheep at the Shepherd's Right

I was a stranger and you invited me in.

MATTHEW 25:35

*D*uring our hectic, busy lives we are clearly focused on our responsibilities. We zoom from one schedule to the next to accomplish our tasks. We do not like to be disturbed. We do not like to be slowed down. But Jesus seems to try and divert our attention. He seems to ask us to stop our important work and do some of his important work when we least expect it.

I was driving on Interstate 80 early in the morning, trying to beat the traffic jams, trying to arrive at work early to finish a project. The speedometer read sixty-five miles per hour. I had a full tank of gas. The car was brand-new, shining, sporting a fresh smell and a smooth running engine.

Suddenly, in the distance I saw, to the side of the highway, a collection of people. The closer I zoomed toward them, the more I realized they had car trouble.

I raced past them, intent on beating the traffic and completing my task at work, but then I looked in the rearview mirror as the people waving their hands grew smaller and smaller. I slowed down, pulled to the side of the highway, and backed up to the stranded people.

It turned out to be what looked like a family: a woman in a dark kerchief, four children sitting on the guardrail clapping their hands to the beat of a song, and the father standing in front of the open hood of his fifteen-year-old car which, obviously, wasn't working.

"Do you know car?" the man asked in broken English.

The wife smiled. She was missing many teeth. One of the boys, the older one, stepped up and said with a shy manner, "We are going to visit my uncle. The car stopped. He's getting married this morning."

Married? On a weekday? In the morning? I don't think so. But I did take a look at the old engine. I know absolutely nothing about cars.

"Can you fix?" the father asked. "My brother is married this morning soon."

I looked up and down the empty highway hoping to see a police car, a tow truck, anyone who might be able to help. Then I looked at the family.

"Where is the wedding?"

"Ten miles over the mountain," the wife said with another smile.

I arrived at work four hours late that morning.

"What happened?" my supervisor asked.

"Well, I went to a wedding."

Three weeks later I received in the mail a postcard from the Bahamas from the groom. It read, in part, "Thank you for my brother. His car is good again. My wife, she is going to name our first son 'Christopher.' Good-bye."

No work is more valuable than helping a person in need for that person is always Christ, and he will always reward you for your generosity.

Tumble down and I fall. Tumble down and I cry out in pain. Tumble down and I look up for an extended hand, for a soothing voice. Thank you, Lord, for when I am weak, you lift me up and invite me into your heart, the home of all healing.

What God Wants You to Do

Your will be done.

MATTHEW 6:10

When I was a high school student I spent an afternoon with a friend in Canada who ran a bookmobile for the rural poor in the eastern section of Ontario. I rode up front with the young volunteer.

I'll never forget driving in a heavy rainstorm. We drove for twenty minutes until we stumbled upon a farm set down in a bleak valley. My driver friend shifted gears as the truck groaned and slowly shook down this long, mud-filled road toward a small, single house.

As we drove down the hill, I saw to my left a man and two children all bending over the ground tending to the crops. I didn't know what they were doing in the rain.

My friend in the bookmobile pressed the truck's horn which sent the children running toward the house. The man stood up straight, placed his hands on his hips, wiped his forehead, then returned to his squatting position and continued working in the field.

A woman greeted us at the door and invited us in.

I had never seen a dirt floor. The two children, a boy and a girl, both under twelve years old, held books in their hands.

"We're done with these," the girl said.

"I'd like another one about hawks," the boy chimed in.

I looked at these children and thought about the carpets in my parents' home, about the books my aunt sent from Belgium which

I never bothered to read.

I became a writer partly because of those two children holding up their books with dirt on their hands. It was then that I saw the power of the written word.

It seems as if God gives us hints each day about what he'd like us to do. If you look closely around you, or if you listen carefully to what a friend says, I bet you will recognize a potential hint as to what God would like you to do. Perhaps it is as simple of an act as dragging in the neighbor's garbage can, or visiting an old aunt who just says on the phone, "Oh, I'm okay, I guess. It is so cold outside." Perhaps she is really saying "I'd love a little company today."

Listen carefully. Observe. God is pointing the direction.

Who tells us there is fruit to be plucked from the tree of life? Who tells us there is water to drink from the well of eternity? Who explains there is work to be done in the field of the Lord? You, my God. I listen and I will act today and all my days for your will and pleasure.

God's Secrets

The secret of the kingdom of God has been given to you. But to those on the outside everything is said in parables.

MARK 4:11

Early one morning, after struggling to wake up, shower, dress, and to slouch toward the orange juice and cereal, I looked out the kitchen window. Sunrise, dew, neighbor's house, forsythia bushes, robin on the grass. If I had been more awake, I would have realized immediately that robins do not have beards; however, at first I was convinced that this particular robin sprouted a fine, brown beard.

How odd to see something out of the ordinary, in the most unlikely places. I recently read about some college students who dismantled a campus police car and reassembled it on the roof of one of the academic buildings.

Well, my full consciousness began to spread thorough my body, as I realized, of course, robins do not have beards. Wings. Red breasts. Feet. Eyes. Then I understood the robin had a mouthful of dried grass.

She's building a nest, I thought.

I learned long ago that if I wait long enough, eventually what I watch will eventually lead me to a conclusion, or to a destination, or to home. Scientists, pilots, and lonely people all recognize this truth.

So I watched the robin peck at the dry grass a bit, pick up a few more thin strands, look to the left, then to the right. (She didn't look in the kitchen.) Then she pushed off and pressed her wings into the air and disappeared instantly in the forsythia bush three feet above where she originally stood.

After a busy day at work, I parked the car in the driveway, walked up the brick steps into the kitchen. The children greeted me at the door.

"I've got a secret," I announced.

"Are we going to the shore?" Karen asked. She often equates secrets to a surprise trip.

"Are we gonna have pizza?" Michael asked.

My teenage son just rolled his eyes thinking "Another of Dad's *great* secrets."

"Follow me," I whispered as I stepped out of the kitchen and back to the driveway. "Over here. Don't tell anyone."

We gathered before the forsythia and I pointed to the nest deep within the green bush. "There's a nest," I announced.

David rolled his eyes. Karen was disappointed we weren't going to the shore, but she was interested in the nest. Michael asked, "Is there an egg?"

I didn't know, so I lifted Michael as he stretched his neck, pulled back a few green branches. "Nope. No eggs." This news convinced Karen that the shore was definitely the better secret; David was already back in the house.

The next morning, after a desperate lunge out of bed, after my shower, after dressing and eating breakfast, I stumbled through my near sleep and out the back door and began to walk toward the car. Just before I stepped into the car, I had a thought. I walked back up the driveway, walked on the grass and stood before the forsythia. I reached in, pulled a few branches back, stood on my toes and peered in. One blue egg.

That night, after work, I entered the kitchen with the newspaper under my arm as the children called out, "Daddy's home."

As I stooped down among my three children I whispered, "I've got a secret!"

We have to be open to the hidden things that are placed before us. We need to pay close attention to the gifts that appear in simple disguises.

In this new day remember that you are a child of God standing before his watchful eye. I believe he hopes that you will discover his secrets, as children discover new things each day. Be open to God's gifts. They need to be unwrapped, discovered, and appreciated.

Think how odd it is when Jesus says that the first will be last. There is a secret there. Think about the parable of how the good seeds will grow on good ground. There is a secret there. I believe the secret is the divine gift from God. He is everywhere, hidden in the bud of a spring flower, and revealed in splendor in the laughter of your neighbor.

I believe I am a mystery, Lord, closed within my body and heart. I believe this mystery is today's frontier, the place for you, my God, to enter and reveal who I truly am. I take your hand and dare step out of my mask and share my faith with those I will greet today in the reality of love.

Wisdom Is From God

Pay attention and listen to the sayings of the wise; apply your heart to what I teach, for it is pleasing when you keep them in your heart and have all of them ready on your lips.

PROVERBS 22:17-18

I remember walking between the academic buildings with the head of the Theology Department, Father Gerald Dolan. It was the fall of 1970, and I was a sophomore at St. Bonaventure University in Olean, New York.

"Look, Christopher," Father Gerald said as he pointed toward the hills that surrounded the campus. His arms stretched out and the sleeve of his brown, Franciscan robe drooped down from his strong arm.

We stopped our walk and both looked toward the place where he was pointing.

"I like so much when the leaves begin to change colors. See how the light passes through the trees at the very top of the hills?"

I tried to see what he saw without much success.

"I like the new gaps between the trees. They always tell me the new season is really upon us."

Now that I look back at that simple exchange of words, I see this was one of the first times that I was in the presence of greatness outside my own love for my father and mother and for my family.

I was a lonely and frightened young man during my first years in college. I was homesick, an average student struggling to understand the many images of beauty and ugliness that surrounded me, and that surround all college students. It was difficult for me to match those things of my home and heart with a world I didn't know was waiting for me.

And there was Father Dolan, a man dressed in one of the most ancient and humble garments: a loose cloth held together with a rope. There was a man who loved God and recognized the obvious beauty of the season moving toward winter.

"Each year, I look for the moment when the gaps between the trees appear."

Over twenty years later I still remember that fifteen-second exchange of words with Father Dolan in the southwestern region of New York State. He was, for me, a part of my own beginning toward greatness I can only hope to attain.

There are people who walk among us pointing toward the light that seeps between the gaps of the tall trees.

Don't you feel God's hand on your shoulder when you need him most? Don't you receive a reassuring word from God when you doubt your own future? Perhaps you know a young person in need of guidance, a reassuring word, a pat on the back.

To accept Christ into our hearts is to accept our need for his love. To guide and to love, we need to be guided and loved. Seek out those who can now benefit from what God has given you.

Let wisdom accumulate in my heart, Lord; let the right words be ready at my lips for those who seek my advice.

Drawn Swords

His speech is smooth as butter, yet war is in his heart; his words are more soothing than oil, yet they are drawn swords.

PSALM 55:21

I stood in line at the food market waiting to pay for my loaf of bread and gallon of milk. Over in the next aisle another long line of people waited to pay for their groceries. My eyes wandered from the cashier, to the magazine rack, to the advertisements hanging on the large windows of the store.

Then I happened to watch a woman, perhaps in her fifties, push her cart up to the adjacent cashier and begin to place the items onto the black, rolling conveyor belt.

If you look closely at what goes on around you, you never know what you will learn.

As the cashier struck the cream-colored keys on her machine, adding up the cost for the different items, the customer placed a coupon upon a can of coffee. The food made its way along the conveyor belt.

The customer began to look around for a moment. She stopped pulling the food out of her cart and she waited. I was curious about what she was, or seemed to be, waiting for.

The cashier reached for the coupon and for the coffee.

"This coupon is outdated," the cashier said in a harsh, triumphant voice.

"Oh, really?" the customer replied, projecting an air of innocence, with a nasty voice of indignation, revealing that she knew all along that the coupon was, indeed, outdated.

I do not fully understand why people are so cruel to each other. I do not fully understand why people try to take, take, take.

How do we expect our world of nations to join hands and celebrate when two women at the checkout line in the corner grocery store battle with sneers on their faces for the right to fifteen cents?

Jesus is our Father. When asked what we ought to do in the world, he said that we should love one another. Each day we have a personal opportunity to be like Jesus and bridge the gap between ourselves and those we seem to dislike.

Perhaps there is someone you dislike but whom you have to see each day. What would happen if you sent that person a small card of greeting? What would happen if you invited that person out for a cup of coffee? What would happen if you bought that person a flower? God would smile. That's what would happen.

Today you can contribute to true peace on earth, and good will toward all people.

Lord, I pray that I may love my enemies, that I may turn my other cheek to those who strike me. I pray that I may extend my hand in friendship and conciliation to those who have lifted their swords against me. Protect me, God, in this treaty of the heart.

Giving Cheerfully

God loves a cheerful giver.

Our cat sits on the deck and sleeps. When she hears the rustle of leaves, or the cry of the mockingbird, she quickly lifts her head up, surveys the advisability to pursue the sound, then she stretches a bit, curls up, and returns to her sleep.

We human beings also sit up and take note at certain times. For example, I stayed up until after midnight writing and proofreading. The time moved without my say-so. When I looked up at the round clock it seemed as if it was laughing, having played a good trick on me, those hands spinning around the numbers without my noticing.

I slept poorly that night, woke up early, drove to work, and acted out the day bravely. When I returned home in the late afternoon, David asked me if I would drive him to the music store because a string on his guitar broke. So I drove him.

When we returned, Roe asked if I would set the table and pick up Karen at her friend's house. I pulled out the glasses and plates and forks and knives and arranged them on the table, then I drove across town. When Karen stepped into the car, she asked if I would take her to the library because she needed a few books for her report on Kentucky.

The librarian reminded me that I had three books overdue.

By the time Karen and I returned to the house, dinner was ready.

Michael asked me if I would help him carry his chair from the living room to the kitchen.

"I used the chair as my helicopter, Dad."

I wanted to ask him if he could have flown the chair back into the kitchen, but I was too tired.

After dinner Roe and I washed and dried the dishes, then she asked me if I would like to go for a walk.

We walked, or, I should say, Roe walked and I marched step-by-step in a steady rhythm, otherwise I would have fallen over and slept on the next, soft lawn.

In the past thirty-six hours I had slept only six hours, and I was exhausted. When we returned from our walk I had to break up an argument between the boys, give Karen a shower, feed the cat, open the door for the cat, wash out the fish bowl, return a call to the insurance agent, read to Karen, and, finally, read to Michael. David, being the oldest, doesn't want me to read to him in the evenings any longer.

I read to Karen, tucked her in, brought her a glass of water, said prayers, chased the ghosts from her closet, pulled down the blinds, kissed her good night.

I read to Michael, tucked him in, brought him a glass of water, said prayers, chased the pirates out of his closet, pulled down the blinds, kissed him good night. I was five seconds away from ending the day and throwing myself onto my bed for the night when Michael said in a quiet voice, "Daddy? Could you get my blanket?"

I wonder if, after Michaelangelo was washing his paintbrushes after having just completed the ceiling mural in the Sistine Chapel, the pope leaned over his shoulder and said, "Michael, I was wondering if you could add just one more image, something like God and man nearly touching. Something like that."

My Michael wanted his blanket which was not on the first floor, but was in the basement, in the back, inside the closet, under the basket. "Karen hid it on me," Michael explained.

I wobbled down the first flight of stairs. I rubbed my eyes. I wobbled down the second flight of stairs and nearly tripped over the cat.

I staggered into the basement, forced my arm to reach into the closet, pulled the blanket out from under the basket. Sleep. Sleep. All I wanted was sleep.

I climbed both flights of stairs as if my legs were made of cement. I stepped into Michael's room, placed the blanket beside him and kissed him good night. Just as I was about to tumble out of his room, he whispered, "Daddy, thank you for going all the way down in the basement for my blanket."

I poked my head up just like the cat does when it hears a rustle in the bushes or hears a mockingbird sing and I said, "Thank you Michael. I love you."

"I love you too, Daddy," and then I walked into my bedroom, flopped on my bed, stretched a bit, curled up, and went to sleep. I wouldn't be surprised if Roe told me the next morning that she heard me purring all night.

How do you give? Freely or from coercion? And what is your motivation? You will be offered many opportunities today to be a giving person, to have a generous heart. Think before you act: am I giving cheerfully or begrudgingly? And do I remember who is watching?

God, Creator of all things, you have given me life, earth, love. You have given me such gifts in your generosity. Today I pray that I may take up your example and give of myself willingly. Help me, Lord, to see who will benefit from my gifts. I pray that I may offer my assistance with joy.

The Garden of God's Delight

Let the fields be jubilant, and everything in them! Then the trees of the forest will sing, they will sing for joy before the Lord.

1 CHRONICLES 16:32-33

Roe and I often walk after supper: down the street to the left, through a small path, along the empty roads winding between maple trees and wild grass. At first these walks were for health reasons. We thought the exercise worthwhile.

During the first week we concentrated on our speed and arm movements. We bought proper walking shoes, wore shorts and loose shirts. In the evenings we dressed in white or yellow.

By the end of the second week, we discovered something beyond the measuring of our pulse: each other. One evening we counted the number of rabbits we came across: eight. Another night Roe and I planned Karen's birthday party. One late afternoon we spoke about our favorite ice cream: chocolate. We compared different brands, textures, prices. I prefer soft ice cream; Roe likes hard ice cream, in a cone, a sugar cone.

By the third week we gave up trying to swing our arms in a true walker's swing. We were holding hands.

Last week, during one of our walks, Roe suddenly said, "Smell! Take a deep breath! What do you smell?"

"Fresh air?" I asked.

"Try again."

I tried again. "Freshly cut grass?"

"We have to turn back a few steps. It's gone now." She stopped,

49

turned around and began walking in the opposite direction. I followed.

"Here! Here it is again! What do you smell?"

I stood next to Roe and brought a barrel full of air into my lungs.

"Honeysuckle?" I asked.

"Yes! Can you smell it?"

Roe and I met when she was twenty-two and I was twenty-four. We both grew up near the edge of woods which were lined with honeysuckle, and the smell of this wild flower brought the same memory to us: the moment of a childhood pleasure in a long-ago adventure through the neighborhood of our separate dreams.

"Let's see if we can find the flowers," Roe suggested. She began to walk upwind, thinking, rightly, that the scent was carried along the slight currents of air moving against us.

Within a few moments we both stood before a small clump of trees, and at the foot of the trees, in shy repose, sat a honeysuckle plant. Roe leaned over and, like a mother plucking a strand of hair from her daughter's face, picked a honeysuckle flower and placed it under my nose.

"Smell," she whispered.

I drew in the breath of a little god hidden deep within the slender petals and smelled the flower.

Perhaps the fountain of youth draws its power from the pressed juices of the honeysuckle plant, for as I recognized the flower's scent, I was back in the yard of my childhood, stopping between a hide-and-seek game with my brothers and sisters, or on my way after a call to supper from my grandmother waving at the top of the back porch steps.

I leaned over the bush, picked a flower and placed it under Roe's nose, and she too closed her eyes.

When we both returned to our senses, we snapped a few long strands of honeysuckle from the plant, then we walked home.

So far Roe and I have both lost ten pounds.

We need to share little things with those we love, for in this sharing, we discover more about those we love. God provides us with a huge exhibit in his World's Fair.

Take a friend out for lunch today and walk together. Enjoy the different displays God arranged for your admiration: flowers, rabbits, trees, smells. Tell your friend how beautiful these God-created things are. Your friend will be grateful for your vision and for your company.

I pray that I may be jubilant in the presence of all God's gifts, that I may sing in the halls of God's house: his earth, his garden, his holy place for my joy. Let me be jubilant.

Precious Memories

"Peace, peace, to those far and near," says the Lord.
ISAIAH 57:19

*W*hen we were children my neighbor Albert and I created a song: "Pickles and alligators out on the lawn. Who's gonna fight 'um before they're gone."

It all started when Albert's mother bought a jar of dill pickles. I had never eaten a dill pickle before. Albert called me into the kitchen and pointed to the counter. "Chrissy look at the jar of baby alligators."

Everyone in the neighborhood knew that I had a dangerous imagination: dangerous to me. I believed anything I was told.

I couldn't understand why anyone would want to place alligators in a bottle, and I was even more disturbed that Albert's mother would buy such a thing in the market.

"Ah, that's not alligators," I said with much courage and authority. Eight-year-old boys know how to defend their notions with courage and authority.

"They are too!" Albert snickered.

"You old goat," I said and walked out of the house, out the back porch, and down the stairs to the lawn. By the time I stepped on the grass, Albert was out on the porch eating an alligator. He had another one in his right hand.

"Pickles and alligators out on the lawn! Who's gonna fight 'um before they're gone!" Albert teased, then he threw the pickled alligator at me. It hit my shoulder and bounced onto the grass.

"That's no alligator," I said. "It looks like a cucumber."

Albert smiled, then took a crunching bite from his pickle. I picked up the pickle he tossed at me and took a small nibble. I winced at the first taste, then I broke off another piece with my teeth and began chewing.

"Not bad," I said.

For years, whenever Albert and I began an argument, we'd end up chanting together "Pickles and alligators out on the lawn. Who's gonna fight 'um before they're gone."

After the publication of my third book, I received a letter from Paris. Albert had become a graphic designer for a French advertising firm. I hadn't heard from him in over twenty years. He said he was browsing in an English bookstore and stumbled across my book. This, in part, is what he wrote:

Dear Chris:

By chance I found your book this afternoon and I felt compelled to write. Since I left the United States I married, divorced, lost time, drew myself into an advertising position here in Paris. My ex-wife and our two children, boys, returned to America and are living somewhere in California, or so I imagine. Your book, *Only the Heart Knows How to Find Them: Precious Memories for a Faithless Time*, reminded me that I, too, had many good memories both in my adult world and in my time when we were young and throwing pickles at each other. I cherish my childhood memories, some of which included you and your brothers and sisters. I will not have the opportunity to watch my own two sons grow up, mostly because of my fault: infidelity and drinking mostly. Jeannette (my ex-wife) remarried. The last letter I received from her included a photograph of the boys and their adopted father out at a baseball stadium. I have terrible regrets, but believe the children will be happier within a stable marriage.

Sometimes I wish I could go back in time and try to rearrange my life into a different pattern, but I am too closely tied to my selfishness and less sober ways that, at this point, I just accept my faults and have a difficult time dulling the pain. Your book helped.

Pickles and alligators out on the lawn. Who's gonna fight 'um before they're gone?

Sincerely,
Albert

Dostoyevsky, in his novel *The Brothers Karamazov*, wrote "There are no memories more precious than those of early childhood in one's first home." These memories sustain us as we grow older.

Like God's promise at the time of our baptism, we are filled with important notions when we are young. In baptism we are blessed with the holy water of past and present acts of faith. We are anointed with God's promise that we will be saved. This symbol can protect us always, just as precious memories protect us and guide us in our times of loneliness or confusion or fear.

Why don't you think back today to some of your comfortable memories, and think about the time God gently poured the cool water of salvation upon your forehead. These thoughts will brighten your day.

I remember the songs of my youth, I remember the sounds of many voices. I remember my schools and teachers. I will not forget the times of comfort. I will not forget the times of joy. And Lord, God, I remember you from my past, embrace you today, and rejoice in the knowledge that you will still be there for me in the future.

The Memory of God's Gift

I tell you the truth, today you will be with me in paradise.

LUKE 23:43

*M*y wife and I bought our little house twenty-six years ago. We moved in during the month of October. The leaves in the tall oak trees had already begun to change into their deep red colors. We didn't know that under the cold autumn earth a small surprise waited for us.

I grew up in a house that was surrounded with a rough garden. I call it rough for there was little difference between the yard and the distant woods and open fields. My father planted ferns, that grew wild at the lip of the woods. He planted raspberry bushes that grew and grew and took control of the entire north side of the property. The daffodils which bloomed each spring were planted by the previous owners of the house. And my grandfather planted white roses that clung to the trellis he built the last summer before his death.

There was one particular flower I made a point of looking for each spring: the bleeding hearts. I thought my mother made up the name. I was startled to see the small, pink flowers which grew in the shape of hearts, just like on the playing cards. Just like on the pictures of *Alice in Wonderland*. I liked to pick a single heart-shaped flower and hold it between my fingers. I liked to pick apart the flower and find its small, white skeleton inside, or at least that is what the inside of the flower looked like.

One afternoon, during our first spring together in our new

house, I was walking in our small yard when I saw, from a distance, a cluster of pink flowers drooping from a green stem: bleeding hearts. I had never seen these flowers anywhere else except in my parents' yard, and here I was, in the yard of my new life with my new wife, and there, waiting for me, were the flowers of my childhood.

I picked one flower and slowly pulled it apart and there, as always, was the inner, white skeleton also shaped like a heart.

We all come from the same roots, from the same soil. We all come from the first love created in a distant garden, or distant desire to be less lonely. How familiar those bleeding hearts were to me. They were simple gifts from God. As is written in Psalm 77:11, "I will remember the deeds of the Lord; yes, I will remember your miracles of long ago." The flowers in my garden were just like miracles, a gift from God plucked, it seemed, from the garden of my childhood.

Look around in your home today and see what gifts God brought to you. Is it a plant? Is it a photograph? Perhaps one of God's gifts is a particular window in your house that brings in much sunlight.

Select a specific gift you recognize as being a true gift from God, then share that gift with a friend today.

In my vision of heaven there is a whole field of bleeding hearts waiting for me.

With my hands I hold little gifts that bring me joy: flowers, a ring, perhaps a favorite book. With my heart I hold big gifts that bring me joy: faith, love, and charity. I pray, Lord, that I may be a little gift in your hands, and a big gift in your heart in all that I think, in all that I say, and in all that I do.

Things Work Out for the Best

It is fine to be zealous, provided the purpose is good.

GALATIANS 4:18

The plan was a trip to the shore for the afternoon. Eighty degrees. Suntan lotion. Picnic lunch. The children ran around the house anxious to dodge the ocean waves again. I dreaded the impending adventure. I do not like sitting in the sun. It hurts my eyes when I try to read. It burns my skin.

"Roe," I called out as I began walking out the door, "I'm going to see if I can buy a beach umbrella."

The first store ran out. None in stock. The second store had too high prices. Finally at the third store I found the umbrella and the price I liked.

After I bought the umbrella, the one with blue and yellow fish, I carried it to my car in the middle of the shopping mall. I wanted to make sure the umbrella was the proper size, and wasn't damaged in any way, so I slipped it out of the plastic carrying case, struggled with the catch, then, like a happy mushroom in the moist woods, the umbrella popped open.

Perhaps I looked like a crazed Mary Poppins in the middle of the parking lot. A woman with five children in her van slowly drove by. The children looked out the window and stared. I winked and danced a bit for the children, a dancing bear in the parking lot with his umbrella and his audience. The children in the car laughed. The woman pressed the accelerator and zoomed off. I waved to the distant children, and they waved back.

When I returned to the house, everyone was ready to pack the car and be off.

An hour and a half later Roe, the children, and I were carrying towels, buckets, blankets, and a picnic cooler along the hot sand. I carried my blue and yellow umbrella.

The only problem about the New Jersey shore in May is the wind. And the only problem about the wind in May is the cold.

I dug a deep hole, jammed the umbrella rod into the ground and packed the sand around the base. Then I sat in the shade with my newspaper, prepared to enjoy the next few hours reading.

The wind suddenly lifted the umbrella out from the hole and carried it off several yards down the beach until I was able to catch up with it. The children laughed and laughed. I looked at them, did a little dance, and they laughed some more.

I held the umbrella high over my head and asked my three children to follow close behind as we played follow the leader. Over the dunes, around the snack stand, down the ramp, to the waves, into the waves they followed me and my umbrella. Roe was embarrassed. The children groaned when I started to sing. Perhaps the seagulls were impressed for they certainly squawked a great deal.

That night, after the children were carried to their rooms, after they were asleep, and as Roe and I were in bed I whispered, "Great umbrella."

Things don't always turn out the way we expect them to, but if we live our lives according to God's wishes things turn out for the best.

Live according to God's commandments, and then tonight, before you sleep, recall what happened today and take notice how an event worked out in a different way than you expected. Notice how the final outcome was really pretty good.

All happiness, Lord, is your history, your book of time spread out before me for my living. Thank you for including me in your pages so that I may see my part in your story. I sing praise to you, my God, author of eternal joy.

Well Seasoned Speech

You shall not misuse the name of the Lord your God, for the Lord
will not hold anyone guiltless who misuses his name.

Exodus 20:7

*W*hen I was a graduate student, a friend of mine called up
on the telephone when I was in my dorm one afternoon and
asked if I would mind taking care of his parrot for a few days while
he flew west on a business trip.

"I'll be back in a week. All Sergeant needs is a banana, some
oranges, and water."

After I agreed to take the bird, my friend arrived at the university
a few hours later with Sergeant, a blue and red macaw parrot sitting
on its perch in the middle of a brass cage.

"I brought some sunflower seeds too. You could cover his cage at
night if you like. He doesn't need much else."

After my friend placed the cage on my bookshelf, we talked for
a few moments about his trip, then he stepped to the door, after he
pulled out seven bananas from a brown bag. "He's been fed for the
day. He won't need anything until tomorrow morning."

"I'm sure we'll be fine," I said as I wished my friend good luck.
"I'll see you in a week."

My friend was off, and I sat at my desk and began my studies for
the evening.

At about eleven-thirty I was tired. I rolled out my paper from the
typewriter, placed my work in a folder, stretched my arms above my

head, closed my desk lamp, and walked over to the small refrigerator in the corner of my room in a hunt for a snack. The bird sat as still as stone in his cage and blinked a few times.

I ate a bowl of cereal, drank a glass of milk, flicked off the ceiling light, and walked to my room. It had been a long day.

It was easy to fall asleep quickly when I was younger. I didn't consider myself to be a writer. I wasn't married. I didn't have children. False dreams put me to sleep quickly. The dreams of my wife and children today cause me many difficult entries to sleep, not out of worry, but out of joy, puzzlement, and wonder.

"Jesus Christ! Jesus Christ! Jesus Christ!"

It was one or two o'clock in the morning. I had been asleep for a couple of hours.

"Jesus Christ!"

I was awoken with these two, distinctly pronounced words. I looked over at my clock radio. The time was illuminated in a fog-like green.

"Jesus Christ!"

Again I heard the words, so I stepped out of bed, and walked across my room, past my silent typewriter to the door. I snapped on the light and there was Sergeant sitting in his cage trying to pull a banana through the narrow bars of the cage. I didn't realize the bananas were sitting on the bookshelf within reach of the bird's claw.

Sergeant looked at me, then bobbed his head up and down a few times. I pried the banana out from between the bars, peeled back the skin and broke off a piece of the fruit and handed it to Sergeant. He pulled it into the cage with his beak, held it in his claw, and began slowly eating the banana. I sat next to him, eating the other part of the banana. Sergeant and I in the middle of a Manhattan college dormitory. I was in my underwear. Sergeant shook his blue and red wings a bit.

I thought about Sergeant. He belonged in a tropical jungle somewhere, sitting up in a lush tree. I didn't know where I belonged.

"Jesus Christ," he said again.

I have read biographies of the saints, read the Old and New Testament. Many college professors spoke about God and the Greeks, the Orient and stars. I didn't expect the Good News to be delivered to me via Sergeant the parrot.

A few weeks after my friend returned from his trip and brought Sergeant home, he called me on the telephone.

"Chris, I'd like to thank you again for taking care of my parrot."

"Oh, that's okay. I enjoyed doing it."

"There's one thing, though," my friend said. "Now, whenever Sergeant is hungry he calls out something that sounds like 'Alleluia?'"

Sergeant and I believed in responsorial hymns.

In Colossians 4:6 it is written, "Let your conversation be always full of grace." Can you grace your spouse, child, colleague, or neighbor with a conversation filled with charm, goodness, honesty, and joy? When Christ asks us not to misuse his name, I believe he is asking us not to misuse the beauty of our speaking gifts. It is too easy to pepper our conversations with swear words and vulgarities that detract from the music of our languages.

In the name of Jesus Christ try and speak with another human being today and listen carefully. See if you cannot hear how, the more you carry on the conversation, the more it sounds like a hymn.

Alleluia! Alleluia! Alleluia to the risen Lord. You are with me. You have kissed me. You have given me your holy name. You have identified yourself to me, oh Lord, so that I may know you, so that I may follow you. I will protect our friendship. I will guard your name. Thank you for the introduction. Alleluia.

The Meaning of Inner Peace

The Lord turn his face toward you and give you peace.

NUMBERS 6:26

There have been a number of moments in my life when I recognized the existence of inner peace. We seek what brings us satisfaction: the success of our children, the love of our wives, husbands, friends, a project well done. Isn't there, however, something more beyond these obvious, well-earned victories?

During an oncoming thunderstorm Johnny and I were riding our bicycles home from the summer lake. Johnny was my neighbor and my best friend when I was a boy.

The clouds blackened. The winds picked up. "We better hurry!" Johnny said as he turned his head and called back to me as I tried to keep up with him, Johnny the strong, Johnny the owner of a beautiful bike, Johnny my friend.

I began to press my feet hard against the bicycle pedals. We reached an incline in the road and coasted with great speed, trying to outrun the storm, the dark storm, the boy-storm, the power that was about to fall upon our heads if we lost the race.

"Hurry up, Chris!" Johnny yelled as he turned down Ivers Place.

This was the moment I recognized happiness: riding my bicycle in the wind with my friend, rushing home to what was safe and dry and stable.

Another time I felt an inner peace was the day I was walking to the Gulf station to pick up my car. It needed an oil change.

The day was warm. The sun was bright. I remember looking at the sky through the trees above my head. My wife and children were home. I was on my way. My hands were in my pocket. I felt somehow like a seafarer upon the world, free, ready to hoist my sails and take stock of my provisions. I felt I could have discovered the Pacific Ocean. Then I saw the gas station sign in the distance, and my reverie disappeared. But I remember the feeling.

Robert Frost spoke about the notion of casting out in many of his poems. Most of his poems have a person in it, and many of those poems deal with people walking out to the field, jumping out from a tree, pushing off, sending themselves into another world. Often, many of the people in those poems also return after the journey is done.

It is in the drifting away from what we know and love that we discover hints of peace. Perhaps that sounds foolish. How can there be peace away from those we love? I suspect it isn't the distance from those we love that creates the inner joy ... it is the realization that we can go home again, that we can take the ride with Johnny once again after the storm. It is the knowledge that we can take that walk to the gas station and turn around and rejoin what we love.

Perhaps the journey of our death begins with this sense of inner peace, a stepping away from life and love toward salvation which includes, someday, a return to those we love?

One of the places where I discover consistent, inner joy is in my writing, particularly in the writing of my poetry. It is there that I step away from my family, from my career, from my life as a person with a lawnmower and three children, and I am a voice of what has been created over twenty years, a sound of myself singing where there is no song, dancing where there is no dance, dividing my dreams into pockets of passion where there is no passion, but the feeling is there.

Writing poetry must be like writing music: the creation of a sound that is language, developed by listening to other music, by living the music, by accepting the diversity of inner turmoil. We must live in the ordinary world under the gold moon. We have to live in the caves as we hunger for the open fields. We are driven toward what it means to be a human being on the loose, on the way, out racing a storm, inviting Johnny to join us on the deck. "Cast sails! Cast sails! We will claim her power against our bare-chested sails and flee all afternoon before we are called in for supper!"

That is the meaning of inner peace. Children know. Sailors know. Poets and musicians know. Turn yourself over to the run, to the escape, to the gentle walk in the afternoon and recognize just beyond the rooftops is your home, your loved ones, your foundation for living ... and be glad.

God wants us to be glad. It is from him that all gifts of peace are created. Step away from your routine. Walk across the street and look at your home. Have lunch in a different spot in your building. Look at your home or your place of work from another perspective and see if you do not feel an inner peace. See if you do not feel a yearning to go home and embrace those you love. This is what God wants us to do when we stand at a distance from the gates of heaven: look toward God's place with hunger and inner peace.

We will all someday be home.

Lord let there be peace in my heart. Let me create peace in the hearts of others. Lord of peace, Prince of Peace, I look toward you for your invitation. The lions and lambs rest at your feet. Let me do as the lions do; let me do as the sheep do: live in peace in the presence of your care.

Brotherly Love

Be devoted to one another in brotherly love.

ROMANS 12:10

I have an old, old friend who was recently placed in a nursing home. Her husband, a surgeon, died ten years ago and she was no longer able to live alone in her house.

On one of my visits to her new home, a comfortable retirement center, she and I were sitting in her room. I was curious why she looked so sad.

"Well," my friend said, "I've been feeding the blue jays and squirrels out my window here, but then I was told by one of the nurses that I am not allowed to do such a thing."

"Did she give you a reason?"

"No. She just said it wasn't allowed."

After my visit, I kissed her good-bye and walked down the hall to the office. I asked to speak to someone in charge.

A tall, thin man in his late fifties stepped out of his office and asked, "Can I help you?"

"Well, my friend in room eighteen loves to feed the birds and squirrels out her window, and she was told that it was against the rules."

"I'll see what I can do," the man said.

On my next visit, as I pulled into the parking lot, I saw in the middle of the front lawn of the retirement center a new birdbath on the grass, and a new bird feeder on a short pole, and I saw my friend filling the birdbath with a yellow watering can.

Because of an act of kindness and love, an old, old woman was able to, once again, feed God's birds and squirrels.

Jesus wants us to love one another. He will reward us for that love. Remember how Mary, the sister of Lazarus, said, "Lord, if you had been here, my brother would not have died" (Jn 11:21). As a result of Mary's love and faith in God, Jesus proclaimed, "Your brother will rise again" (Jn 11:23). Because of an act of kindness and love, Mary witnessed the glory of God.

Think of a friend who is experiencing discomfort. See if you can't arrange something today so that your friend will be a little bit more comfortable. Your act of kindness and love will be rewarded.

Lord God I inherited from your grace the impulse to do good for others. Please place before me a task so that I may clearly see what is your will today so that I may continue to live off your inheritance.

Vision

What did you go out to see?

MATTHEW 11:8

*I*n third grade, I had x-ray vision. I could look through solid walls and watch my grandmother reading her newspaper at the kitchen table. I could stare down beyond the floorboards and see my father at his workbench in the basement building his sailboat. I could concentrate hard and gaze right into the living room and watch my brother and sister playing Monopoly. I was Superman.

In fifth grade, when I was eleven, I realized that no one could really have x-ray powers, so I settled for Davy Crockett eyes and learned how to toss a tomahawk into a tree with confident accuracy, and read the eye chart in school with 100 percent clarity. The nurse awarded me with a certificate stating that I had perfect 20/20 vision, and this afternoon I came home with my first pair of reading glasses.

I am fifty years old, and I can no longer see as well as I once did. What is happening to me? Boys don't dream about heroes any longer, and machines can see better than I can.

In 1990 the Hubble Telescope was released into the earth's orbit and has been peering around the universe with more power and with more accuracy than Superman and Davy Crockett combined.

The Hubble Telescope is about the size of a school bus. I am about the size of a jelly cabinet. The Hubble telescope weighs 24,500 lbs. I weigh 180 lbs. The Hubble moves at 17,500 miles per hour. It takes me 43 minutes to get out of bed and step into my car for my morning commute. The Hubble Telescope was created to unlock the mysteries of life. I was created to figure out how to pay for the college education of three children. Hubble's giant mirror took three years to grind and polish. My dentist has been grinding and polishing my teeth for forty years and they are still not perfect. The Hubble Telescope can detect images that are nearly four billion times fainter than what we can see. I can't read newspaper print any longer without my new glasses.

They say that in the near future we will be able to create more and more sophisticated telescopes that capture light in such a way that we will be able to see images from the past. Heck, I can already look into the past. If I squint real hard and stare into my bathroom mirror, which wasn't polished by NASA, I can barely see Superman zooming around the dining room table with his bath-towel cape, or I can glimpse Davy Crockett wrestling a cocker spaniel on the back lawn.

After I finished reading the newspaper tonight I, for the first time, like Clark Kent, took off my glasses, but I didn't turn into Superman.

God of all seeing, God of vision, God of sight, cleanse my eyes each morning so that I too may see the glory of your kingdom.

We Are Not Alone

I was lost once in the deep Canadian woods. My father bought two hundred acres two hours west of Ottawa many years ago. When I was a teenager I liked to take risks, though they did not involve drinking, drugs, or sex. My risks were simpler and less complicated, but I was alone just the same.

My parents drove the two miles to the nearest town and left me alone in the cabin for extra vacation sleep. When I woke up I found a note from my mother telling me that she and my father were buying lunch and if I wanted to I could join them at Monique's house, which sat on a hill overlooking a still lake.

I planned to ride my bicycle to Monique's house, but then I ate breakfast, stretched on the couch, and looked out the window.

I had never walked through the complete two hundred acres of rough woods. I wasn't in the mood to see anyone, so I decided to pursue a hike. I filled a canteen with cool well water, slipped on my boots, closed the door behind me, and began my journey.

We often begin to suspect we are taking a risk in life, but then we pull back, fearful of the possible change. I looked toward the dark trees and tangled vines and suddenly imagined myself a little boy about to suspend myself from claws that will entangle me and bring me to a wide mouth to be eaten. But I walked into the woods just the same.

There is a holy and cool moisture that clings to the moss and thick bark which causes the lungs to expand wider with each breath. I had to bow down as I walked to avoid hitting my head on the low branches. There is a certain respect the woods demand.

At one point the trees and brush closed around me with each new step. My way was suddenly slimmer, a narrow hallway pressing in against me from both sides.

The pine needles were soft under my feet, and hard against my cheeks. The thick air drenched me with moisture until I finally emerged in a clearing deep inside the woods. This was one of the first times I thought I heard voices. I knew I was alone, miles away from any human voice, and yet I thought I heard laughter, a man and a woman perhaps, or a boy and a girl. Two people for sure, male and female. I looked up and saw the tips of the trees bending back and forth.

It was not, after all, the language of people, but rather the wind whispering gossip among the pointed trees, perhaps mocking the little boy lost in the woods.

I walked on.

An hour later I began to feel the earth slanting upward, and I leaned my energy into the hill's challenge. The trees were less dense, the field freshly set with wild blueberries. I leaned over like a bear and scooped up the berries with my wide paws, pressing the fruit into my mouth. Perhaps this was Eden. Perhaps this was the place we seek in our attempt to contain peace or the appearance of peace, or a youthful ambition to discover peace.

By the time I reached the top of the hill, I was thirsty. After twisting the black cap from my canteen, I pressed the bottle to my lips and drank nearly all the contents, allowing some of the water to flow down my cheeks and neck.

When I decided it was time to return to the cabin, I couldn't tell what direction I was to take. I walked down the side of the steep hill where I thought I had come, but I didn't find any blueberries.

When I entered the woods, I didn't recognize the trees, or feel the same sweetness against my skin.

My biggest disappointment was my discovering a paved road. Unfortunately there was a road sign just ahead explaining the number of miles to the lake: two, the lake where my parents were to have lunch with Monique.

By the time I arrived on Monique's deck, the dessert had been eaten and everyone was taking turns looking through the binoculars, trying to get a closer look at the two loons courting upon the smooth surface of the lake.

"How was your morning?" my mother asked.

I was embarrassed by the question. How do I tell my mother the trees caressed me, I was drugged on blueberry juice, and drunk on well water?

"Oh, I got lost a bit in the woods."

"Take a look at the loons," my father suggested.

I placed the binoculars to my eyes, adjusted the focus, and found the two birds swimming side by side, and then one gave out its silly, loud, whirling loon cry. Perhaps the loon saw me, lamenting my lost lover: the air and moisture, the berries, the mother-earth.

It is difficult to accept the paved roads we have created for ourselves.

When you think that you are lost, you are really on the right path toward God if you live a life in acceptance that the Lord God is your Savior and protector. He will not abandon you in the deepest moments of your suffering, in your deepest moments of what you may feel is fear and loneliness.

You will find yourself alone sometime today: in the elevator, walking to the mailbox, sitting in the kitchen. Stop for a moment and see if you can feel God's presence, then say aloud, "Hello. Welcome. Thank you for your company. I am not alone."

Bring me word, Lord, that you are near. Bring me comfort so that I may prepare myself for your visit. Hear me in my small voice calling out to you: "I am not lost, Lord, I am not lost but am found in the desert. You have come for me."

Honor Thy Father

Each of you must respect his mother and father.

LEVITICUS 19:3

The furnace in my parents' home was not working properly. Each time it was called upon for heat, it coughed up a miserable sound, then rumbled. After my mother phoned and explained the problem, I stepped into my car and drove the thirty minutes to the house where I grew up. My father had, once again, forgotten to drain the furnace.

My father is eighty-two.

When I pulled into the driveway I was overcome with a feeling of dread and depression. The trees in the yard seemed to droop. The house looked old and worn out. As I entered the foyer, I heard the television blaring in the living room. My father sat in his chair reading the closed captions on the bottom of the TV screen. His hearing aid sat on the table. My mother explained that their cat Misha was dying, and that the vet thought it best that it be put to sleep the next day. The cat was seventeen years old.

I walked down to the basement. It was cold and damp. As I reached for the string that was attached to the single light bulb, I looked around the dim room: workbench, tool board, discarded wood. This was the basement where my father built a twelve-foot sailboat, a fort for my plastic soldiers, and a weaving loom for my sister.

My father was a lawyer.

The tools in the basement were rusted; the workbench was cov-

75

ered with thick dust. I heard the loud television's muffled squawk seeping through the floor above me.

After I opened a valve at the bottom of the furnace, I watched the brown sludge drain into a dry, empty bucket, then I closed the first valve and opened the second, which filled the proper chamber with new water. The water level, which hadn't been checked in weeks, was precariously low.

My father was a college professor.

I turned out the basement light, walked up the creaking stairs, stepped into the kitchen, and helped myself to several grapes from the bowl of fruit that always seemed full. When I was a child, my father held my hand in the fruit market and asked me to help him select the best grapes.

My father tells the story about the day he was released from the prisoner-of-war camp in Belgium during World War II. "I had a bit of money in my pocket, and the first thing I bought was a small bag of grapes. I'll never forget those grapes, so cold and sweet."

My father was an editor.

I walked into the living room with the grapes in my hand. My father leaned out of his chair and tried to adjust his reading glasses. My mother sat on the couch petting the thin, dying cat.

Just as I sat down beside her, my father turned and said, "Christopher, your mother and I took a walk yesterday afternoon through the park, around by the old swamp, and we saw the biggest turtle. Bring the children this weekend and we'll see if we can't find that turtle again." Then he turned to the television and adjusted the color quality.

My father was a writer.

After I kissed my mother good-bye, I left the house, slid into my car and drove off.

Last month my father announced that he has finally given up tennis. "I can't see the ball any longer. The cataract operation didn't help much after all."

That following weekend my father led my wife, our three children, and me on a grand turtle hunt. We walked single file between the dried bulrush plants, jumped over streams, startled six geese, and climbed the park observation deck.

We returned to the house two hours later with pussy willows, apple blossoms, three types of wild violets, and three smiling grandchildren.

As I gave my wife a back rub that night in bed I whispered, "It's sad their cat died."

We didn't see a turtle that weekend, but for a few hours I forgot that my father is an old man. For a few hours I stepped along the outer edges of the swamp and tried to hear the turtle's laugh as I stood upon the spring afternoon with my father expecting nothing more but our being together, and that was good.

I believe that we are born to love. We are born to know the voice of our fathers and mothers. We are born to do our duty according to the father's wishes, according to the mother's wishes. We do honor to our parents in the way we live our lives and in the way we acknowledge with gratitude the love and labor they have invested in our survival.

To honor our fathers and our mothers is to honor God.

Visit the grave of your parents today and say a prayer in thanksgiving for the gift of life they have given you. Or call your parents on the telephone and share a happy childhood memory with them. Perhaps you could mail your father a note. Tell him how much you love God. Tell your mother how much you love her.

God the Father you gave up your only Son to death so that I may live. Jesus, Lord, in your agony, dying, and in your resurrection you have given me life. From the love of my parents I was born. From the love of the Lord we all have been born twice: once in the flesh and once in the spirit. I pray that I may honor life, celebrate life so that my soul shall live according to you, my Father, and your wishes.

Blessed Is the Man in the Snow

Unless you change and become like little children.

MATTHEW 18:3

*O*ften, before I walk upstairs for the night, I look out the back window and flick the switch to the floodlights outside. Over the years I've startled a raccoon climbing up a tree, a skunk digging in the grass for grubs, a number of cats strolling through the darkness.

One particular late evening, after the children were asleep and Roe was sleeping I again turned the back lights on. It was snowing. I like watching the snow fall, suddenly illuminated with my false light.

I noticed this snow accumulated a few inches. I grabbed my coat, quietly opened the back door, turned out the yard lights, and walked to the middle of the lawn.

The houses in the neighborhood looked like dark boxes. The trees loomed over me in an accusing fashion. "You should be in bed," they seemed to say with their crooked, pointing branches.

I stooped to the ground and gathered a handful of snow and licked it. Forty-two-year-old men don't lick the snow. Then I stooped again and rolled a snowball into my hands, pulled my right arm back and let fly my missile and missed the tree I aimed for.

How odd to be in the middle of the lawn, to be in the middle of all the activity of the heavy snowfall and not hear a sound. The silence of the snow.

I looked to my left, then to my right. I checked the empty street, then I fell backwards. I waved my arms up and down, spread my legs open and closed against the snow, then I quickly stood up. A snow angel.

It snowed and it snowed.

I began to feel the cold, then I had a final idea. Once again I stooped down and gathered snow into a ball, but this time I left it on the ground and began to roll it in front of me. Within a few minutes my ball was half my size. A few minutes later the snowball was large enough. I then rolled a second ball, not as large as the first. After I finished rolling the third ball it was the labor of the next few minutes which revealed the sure shape of my snowman.

I reached my hand to the top of my head and plucked my cap and placed it onto the snowman's head, I then began to return to the house.

After I stepped into the house, after I hung up my coat, I walked to the back window, flicked the light on again and there he stood, frozen in midnight, the image of a man with a green cap, motionless in time, pleased to be where he belonged. I waved. The snowman did not wave back.

The next morning I woke up to the sound of my three children hooting and laughing in the backyard. I slouched out of bed, opened the blinds, and saw the children at work building their own snowmen, three children snowmen standing beside the one I built the night before.

I clearly understand how lucky my snowman is. Blessed man in the snow. Holy the children as they sing in the midst of winter.

Snow, like the truth of God, cannot be fully appreciated unless you become, again, like little children.

We often feel that we have to play the role of an adult: on a business trip, at a meeting, on the telephone, at a party of colleagues. People who pretend that they are all adult and not children are false in the eyes of God. There is a difference between being childlike and childish.

We ought to act like the Christ child, innocent before the world in all our power and love which we are willing to share with those who come into our lives.

Laugh aloud today. Invite your boss out for an ice-cream cone. Take your children to the zoo and roar like the lion when you see the lion. Send balloons to your husband. Step outside and spend some time on the rope swing. Kick up your legs and swing back and forth and back and forth and laugh in the shadow of God who knows you as his child.

Always be a child of God, a child of light.

Lord I feel as if I am the same person I was when I was fifteen. I look at myself in the mirror and see an adult, but when I listen to my heart I know I am still the child. Grant me, God, the joy of a child. Help me continue to see what the child sees.

The Protection of God

Because of the tender mercy of our God, by which the rising sun will come to us from heaven to shine on those living in darkness and in the shadow of death.

LUKE 1:78-79

he German troops were advancing into Belgium. We could hear explosions. I was so frightened. 'My arms,' I said to your grandmother. 'My arms! I am afraid that they will shoot off my arms!'"

My mother was a teenager in the spring of 1940, and because she was so frightened she, my grandmother, and my uncle fled their Brussels home, crossed over the French border, and became refugees. They didn't know where they were going except far away from the bombs.

After much travel, after much exhaustion, my uncle Henry, my grandmother, and my mother arrived in a small town on the coast of France: Dunkirk.

"There were so many people: families like us carrying suitcases, children crying, planes flying overhead. And the soldiers. There were thousands of soldiers. We simply thought this was normal, probably what the rest of the world was experiencing at the moment. Of course we didn't know at the time that the British troops were being pushed to the sea and were stranded, waiting for any possible help their country might, and did, send across the channel to rescue them.

"But we were not troops. We were three hungry, tired people in search of a hotel."

Of course my family couldn't find a hotel, and it became obvious to my grandmother that they had to leave this city of turmoil. They walked to the bus station where there were hundreds and hundreds of people waiting for one of the last buses to leave Dunkirk.

Have you ever been in a crowd when suddenly the people from the rear begin to move forward like a wave and all who are in front are shoved?

"When the crowd saw the bus," my mother explained, "the crowd began to push. The bus approached closer and closer and the crowd increased its fury."

My grandmother saw my mother being thrown under the bus, and she screamed and screamed at the bus driver to stop.

Above the roar of the crowd, the driver managed to hear my grandmother's pleading and he stopped the bus.

He stepped out and asked my grandmother what the trouble was.

"My daughter! She's been thrown under the bus!" The driver and my grandmother stooped under the crowd and there was my mother flat on her back with the rear wheels of the bus rolled up on the side of her outstretched dress.

"Then the driver turned to my mother and said, 'Because your daughter had such a fright, your family may have the first seat on the bus.'"

My mother, grandmother, and uncle climbed in. The crowd pressed forward, filling the remaining seats quickly, and the bus drove off leaving most of the other people behind.

So much would have been lost in the history of my family had the wheels rolled six inches more: my brother and sisters, my own life ... my children David, Karen, and Michael.

We are held together with a thin, historical thread of life.

I am sure that God must have wept during World War II. The world seems to cry out at times, "My God, My God, why have you forsaken me?" Chaos, hate, national turmoil is the culmination of lost faith among a whole people. We feel abandoned to evil.

Do not be afraid. In times of your own chaos or inner turmoil do not be afraid to stand up against evil and regain control of your life. Tip your flag of triumph toward God as he stands there waiting for you with his treaties of peace and forgiveness.

God of mercy when I sit in darkness, remind me to call out your name. When I am at battle with pain, remind me to place your hand on my forehead. When I am in doubt, parade the victory of your resurrection in my heart and mind for then I will be reminded.

Choose the Weak

God chose the weak things of the world to shame the strong.
1 CORINTHIANS 1:27

*A*t a recent Little League game I was sitting in the bleachers watching my daughter, Karen, playing the catcher's position.

Halfway through the game a man with one leg hobbled up to the right field fence, leaned his crutches against a trash basket, and held on to the fence for support.

There was much cheering from the crowd as the game continued. Occasionally I looked in the direction of the one-legged man. He wiped his brow. He stooped forward a bit. I noticed he closed his eyes often.

As my daughter returned to the bench between innings, she looked over and waved. I waved back.

Toward the end of the game, I turned to my left and noticed two little girls walking together. They were, perhaps, eight years old. One girl suddenly noticed the one-legged man. She raised her eyebrows, cupped her mouth with her hands, then nudged her friend and pointed. They both laughed.

The closer the girls made their way toward the man, the more amazed they were. At one point one of the girls stooped down to establish, for certain, that the man was, indeed, missing his right leg. When the girl stood up again, she poked her friend, then she lifted her right leg and began hopping. "See, I can do it too," she said, laughing again.

The other girl looked at the man, then she too lifted her leg and hopped along next to her friend. They both continued to laugh. After a moment, they knocked each other off balance, landed on their two good legs, and then they ran together to the snack stand.

"Daddy!" My daughter called out at the end of the game. "We won!" She ran up to me from the field, held my hand as we started walking to the car.

"It was so much fun. Did you see me hit? I also tagged the girl out at home plate. The coach wants to take us all out for ice cream." As Karen spoke about the victory, about her favorite ice cream flavor, and about the winning run, I looked to my right and saw the one-legged man hobbling slowly across the field.

"Daddy? Aren't you listening?" Karen asked.

"Yes, Karen. A fine victory," I said as I thought about the man who comes to watch the children play and listen to their laughter.

We can take great delight in a daughter singing about her baseball victory. It is obvious who the champion is just by looking at the scoreboard. But the old man with one leg is a different type of victor.

In our lives God does not create a clear scoreboard. We have to look closely with Christ's eyes and find the athletes of God's quiet team. "Blessed is he who has regard for the weak; the Lord delivers him in times of trouble" (Ps 41:1).

Seek out the weak, join them in their struggle for then you too can claim a victory.

Lord, God of all strength, help me recognize the true power of the powerless for then I will understand the triumph hidden in my own pain.

Lighting the Way for Others

When Jesus spoke again to the people, he said, "I am the light of the world. Whoever follows me will never walk in darkness, but will have the light of life."

JOHN 8:12

*D*o you hold up a light for those you love so that they may see where they are going? Perhaps they do not know that your arm hurts. Perhaps they do not know that you spend many hours polishing your lantern and wiping the glass so that the best rays of light pierce the darkness.

When I was eight I invented a game with a bottle of bubbles. First I created many bubbles through my plastic blower, then I looked for a bubble that was wider than the lip of the bottle. I chased the bubble, then I caught it with the bottle. The bubble sat on the top, covering the opening. In my mind my bottle of bubbles was now a lamp with its flame.

Of course the "flame" was the bubble. The game was to see how far around the yard I could walk until the bubble popped, or until my "light" was extinguished.

Each time the bubble burst, I ran back to the front steps where I began and started all over again, trying to beat my previous distance with my light game.

If there is a single truth I wish to pass along to my three children, it is this: "I cannot solve all your problems, but I can help you with each and every one of them."

It seems to me that we human beings are built to help each other. We have the ability and the sense to help those in need.

I think about a small boy lighting the yard with his bubbles. I think about the man lighting the path of his children's lives with advice, hugs, suggestions. Those we love best will tend to brush aside our advice quickly, but we do not stop lighting the way just the same.

Today make it a point to offer your gift of advice to someone who is in the dark. Perhaps a coworker is trying to solve a problem. Perhaps your spouse cannot find his or her way out of a sticky social dilemma. Perhaps your high school student doesn't know how to correct a mistake he or she made in school.

What would Jesus do in the streets of Jerusalem if he came upon a person with a difficult decision to make? He would light the way with his words of eternal wisdom. Jesus would encourage the one who is puzzled. Jesus would sit beside your coworker, your spouse, your son or daughter, and he would offer advice based on what he knows.

God's knowledge is complete. If you imitate Christ in your gesture of help, the right words of advice will come to your lips.

Please, Lord, do not walk too far ahead of me in my journey. I do not want to lose track of your light. I choose to live in your light. Let me hold your robe so that I may always see.

Finding Truth

Truth will set you free.

JOHN 8:32

I read in the newspapers this morning that scientists believe the Milky Way is being pulled with a super force away from its common shape. I like to read about things beyond my understanding because these things give me a clear reminder that I am not as clever as I sometimes think I am.

During my work as a school administrator I am often asked to make suggestions on teacher improvement. I am asked by parents what I am doing to improve the reading and writing curriculum.

I can stand before a large crowd of people and make pronouncements, recite statistics, explain a reading and writing philosophy that seems to make sense to everyone around me, but often a more powerful truth is discovered in the most unexpected places.

I met a third grade boy in the library of the elementary school. He was quietly reading.

"What are you reading?" I asked.

"Just a book," the boy answered.

"What is the book about?"

"A boy in a peach, and how he makes friends with these insects."

"Why do you like the book?"

"I don't know. Because I'm the boy in the peach."

I believe it is better to open our eyes and hearts when we wish to learn simple truths. All my fancy college statistics will not move an audience as much as the story of the boy who reads because he believes he is the person in the book. That is what my real job in education is all about: connecting children to books.

St. John wrote that the truth shall make you free. Look around today for images of truth: a cross at the simple tip of a church, your wedding ring, a neighbor's warm wave across the street.

We have more to learn from what is placed before us than from what we seek.

God in heaven, God in my house, because you taught me to love, because you taught me to see, because you taught me to listen, I am free in your truth. I am grateful to be your student.

God and Fairness

Every good and perfect gift is from above, coming down from the
Father of the heavenly lights.

JAMES 1:17

*E*ach year, during the first week of July, David, Karen, Michael, and I open the garage door, adjust our eyes to the darkness, straddle our bicycles, grip the handlebars, adjust our brakes, and zoom down the driveway.

We coast to the stop sign, turn left, ride for three minutes, cross the main street, and peddle down the church driveway.

The driveway is long and wide, bordered by wide lawns, maple trees, and ... wild blackberry bushes, which no one seems to care about.

This past July, my children and I raced along the blacktop, past the sign Our Lady of Good Council Church. We were going blackberry hunting.

Life, in a way, is like picking blackberries. There are plenty of thorns waiting for you, but if you are careful, and delicate, and grateful, and hungry, and patient, the fruit will be your prize.

Michael was ahead of us. "Come on, you guys! Hurry up!"

"The berries won't walk away," Karen shouted.

"I wish they weren't so loud," David said.

Michael laughed in the distance. Karen tried to catch up to him, as he made zooming noises like a rocket or like a nine-year-old boy.

Suddenly all was quiet. Karen and Michael were standing before the bushes. By the time David and I arrived, I had a suspicion.

"There aren't any blackberries," Karen said.

Michael had his hands on his hips. "That's not fair."

David stepped closer to the bushes. "There were a lot of berries, but someone ate them all." He snapped off a piece of the bush to show me the empty stem where, indeed, there once were blackberries.

"Maybe a bear ate them?" Michael asked hopefully.

"Nah," Karen answered. "There aren't any bears around here."

"That's not fair," Michael repeated.

"What's not fair?" I asked.

"We wanted the berries. We come each year. It's our secret. They're our blackberries."

"Well, not really," David said. "This isn't our property."

"Well, it's not a nice thing to do, take them all. It's just not fair," Michael repeated as he climbed on his bicycle and announced, "Race you guys home!"

Three children and a forty-two-year-old man were suddenly in the Tour de France, racing for the finish line. Michael! No David! No Karen! Here we are folks, I think David, no Karen is winning and, and ... I zoomed ahead of everyone and flew into the garage first.

"The winner by a nose!" I called out as I claimed my victory. The children quickly followed, parked their bikes, and ran to the back door where Roe was waiting for them with a full pitcher of iced tea in her right hand.

At the ten o'clock Mass the following Sunday, Fr. Pat spoke about the gifts God has given us, then he said, "And let me tell you about the blackberries."

Well, the children all looked at me.

Fr. Pat continued. "I was walking to the post office. My car wasn't working, so I thought it would be nice to walk. I don't walk much anymore. Just beyond the church I found a beautiful blackberry bush full of plump, ripe blackberries. I remember picking blackberries with my mother when I was a little boy."

Fr. Pat told the story about his mother, then he ended his sermon by saying, "I never got to the post office that day. I stayed in the blackberry patch and ate them all. It was the most fun I'd had all week, and it brought back such memories. God surprises us with all sorts of gifts."

After church, Michael said, "I guess it's fair after all."

When we feel life and God have been unfair because of events that have taken place, we could remember the words of Abraham when he affirmed God's fairness: "Will not the Judge of all the earth do right?" (Gn 18:25).

Take one injustice, however small, that you experience today, and remember these words of Abraham.

Take a moment to thank God that you live under his fair judgment.

Though I do not see the final judgment, though I do not see the trials of all men and women, I do trust in your verdict, Lord. May I come to your court and be judged worthy of your admiration.

God and Loss

A time to be born and a time to die, a time to plant and a time to uproot.

ECCLESIASTES 3:2

*L*ast winter my parents' house suffered under the heavy ice and melting snow. The roof above my father's office began to leak to such a degree that we had to carry his books, desk, and manuscripts up to an empty bedroom.

In early spring the damage was assessed by a local carpenter: the roof, the beams, all would have to be replaced. "And the wisteria vine will have to be cut down."

My father planted the wisteria in 1948, the year my mother and father arrived in America from Europe. During the next forty-five years my parents raised six children, planted raspberries, wrote books, drove back and forth from work, and endured the death of their second child. During the regular habits of their lives, the wisteria silently grew along the side of the house and up to the terrace, year to year, blossom to blossom.

"I can't repair the roof unless the vine is cut down. I've never seen such a vine," the carpenter announced.

My mother and father didn't want to cut the plant. The purple flowers, the smell in spring, the beauty of the long, thick vine. Little can replace such a constant reminder of beauty.

After permission was granted, the carpenter, in less than four minutes, cut the vine and pulled it away from the house. Each minute represented each decade the vine quietly grew.

After the work was complete, I drove to my parents' home to admire their new roof. I walked to the side of the house. The work was professional. There was no more leak. The house recovered from its winter bruise. Then I leaned over and lifted a portion of the great twisted, gray, lifeless vine. Then I looked up and there my mother and father stood on the porch looking down at my catch.

"Your father said he's going to plant a new wisteria on the other side of the house." I nodded, as I tossed the dead plant to the side, and stepped inside the house for a piece of my mother's sponge cake.

Loss and the acceptance of loss is a regular occurrence in our lives. We are built for such loss. We are also built to endure such sadness, but we will endure because we believe in the God of Isaiah who says that one day *our sun will never set again, and our moon will wane no more; the Lord will be our everlasting light, and our days of sorrow will end* (Is 60:20).

If you have recently suffered a small or enormous loss, remember how things used to be until you can smell the purple flowers of the wisteria, and then all will be well again. I promise you.

I weep and pray. I weep and pray. In my sorrow I carry my faith in anticipation of the joy and triumph that has been promised to me by my Lord, Jesus Christ.

Our Thoughts Are Not His Thoughts

Your labor prompted by love.

1 THESSALONIANS 1:3

*D*o you ever have a weekend that has nothing on the calendar, a free weekend to do exactly as you please? When I arrived home from work on a Friday afternoon not long ago, I was greeted by the children excited about their *new* rooms. Roe helped the children rearrange their beds and dressers.

"Come see my room first," Karen said as she tugged my right hand. Michael fell to the floor and screamed, "No! Come see my room first!"

I was pleased it was Friday afternoon. I was looking forward to a peaceful weekend. "Michael, hold my hand and lead me upstairs. We'll see Karen's room first, then yours."

As I walked upstairs, Karen insisted that I close my eyes until I stepped into her room. She wanted me to appreciate the entire effect of the new look. "Okay, Daddy. You can open your eyes now."

Her bed stood where the dresser once stood. Her dresser stood where the bed once stood. "Karen, I love this. Did Mommy help?"

"Yes," my daughter said as she tumbled backwards on her bed and rolled into a ball and giggled.

"Come see my room!" Michael yelled. "Close your eyes."

Once again I was led into a room. "Okay, now open them," Michael laughed.

Again, the bed and dresser were switched. I sat on Michael's bed.

Roe sat on Michael's bed. Michael began bouncing on the bed when I heard a small crack.

"What was that?" Roe asked as she gave the bed an extra bounce. CCCCRACK! The rear portion of the bed collapsed.

I stood up and leaned over and looked at the damage. I was expecting to see a broken leg; instead I saw that the back leg of the bed had broken through the floor.

"I can't believe it! The floor broke!"

Well that is all Karen had to hear. She began to cry. "I don't want to fall through the floor!"

The mind of a child works in reds and yellows; in light and darkness. A child's fear is a combination of fireworks and mysteries.

"Don't worry Karen. Just a small part of the floor broke. It was an accident. I can fix it."

The original builder in 1929 didn't join an oak slat against the floor beam. Instead, the wood was held by the grooves on each side of an adjoining piece of wood. When Roe changed the position of Michael's bed, she just happened to place the rear right leg on the weak section of the floor.

I looked at that hole. Michael wanted to see the whole bed crash through the dining room ceiling. Roe carried Karen downstairs.

Do you remember the scene in the movie "It's a Wonderful Life" where Jimmy Stewart runs up the stairs and grabs the broken part of the banister?

"Yup, yup, yup," I said aloud to no one in particular in my Jimmy Stewart voice. "It's a good thing we don't have anything planned for the weekend."

I stepped out of the bedroom and headed for the basement to see if I had any wood that might fit my weekend project.

My idea for the weekend was to simply relax. This was not God's idea. How do we react when things do not turn out as we intended? Do we become angry? Do we blame God? Take the opportunity today to greet your first unplanned intrusion as a challenge to turn the surprise into a labor of love for God.

Though I work in the fields of my labor, though I toil and carry heavy loads upon my back, I call the field paradise and identify the weight as Christ. Earth is the best place to love the Lord.

Be Cautious in Your Ambition

Fear of the Lord teaches a man wisdom, and humility comes before honor.

PROVERBS 15:33

My father made me a wooden sword from a long piece of pine. I liked the way the tip of the sword was smooth and sanded to a rounded curve, and how it balanced in my hand.

One spring, I and my sword entered the woods behind the house where the skunk cabbage grew and the trees were tall and creaked with each movement of the distant wind.

During my adventures, I kept my sword inside a belt loop of my jeans until I was confronted with the pricker bushes attacking my socks or with the creeping ivy reaching out toward my face.

That afternoon I drew my sword and slashed the bushes and vines. I cut the skunk cabbage at the base of the stem and watched the leaves fall like deflated balloons. A boy alone in the woods likes to believe he is the central power: damming up a stream with stones, pitching acorns at a distant crow, squashing his hard footprint into the soft mud. I was Hercules defending my life against the jack-in-the-pulpits. I was Daniel Boone trying to lure the bear out from under the honeysuckle. I was Merlin turning the bear into my gray cat, which meowed when I called her.

At one point I stood before a dead tree. Its bark was peeling. Its branches were stiff and dry. "This Roman column needs the push from the god of the forest," I called out. I liked to read the Greek and Roman myths when I was eleven.

I leaned against the trunk and began to push my full weight back and forth against the dead tree. Quickly the tree began to sway. It felt like the motion of a horse under me, this movement gaining more and more energy with each exertion from my body.

There was sudden life where there was, moments before, dry wood standing like an erect skeleton. Then I heard a small crack. I continued to rock the tree back and forth accepting my near conquest. From deep within the tree's truck, I could hear more splitting sounds like popping sticks and crackling fire, and then—with a final push—the tree broke at its base with a loud crack and collapsed to the ground.

I drew my sword and crept up to the still serpent and claimed my victory for England and Rome over all that is evil and threatening to little boys as I placed my foot securely on the round trunk.

Then I saw the hole. It was a woodpecker hole, round and dark. I dropped my sword to the ground and stepped up to the tree trunk. I placed my right eye close to the hole and closed my left eye. I could see dried grass.

I placed my index finger into the hole and wiggled my thumb against the outer portion of the tree and pulled and pulled until the outer wall of the tree broke under the pressure of my fingers to reveal the inside of the hole. The light revealed a round ball of grass and seeds and small twigs.

Using my fingers as tweezers, I carefully plucked apart the ball of grass. Small seeds rolled to the ground. Within the center of the nest, I found a dead gray mouse curled up in a ball of ears and legs and tail and fur. The tree's fall hadn't killed the mouse for it was cold and stiff. Perhaps it had frozen in the winter, I thought.

I held the mouse in my outstretched hand. How insignificant I felt. England was suddenly lost. I picked up a flat stone, dug a shallow grave, placed the mouse into the open earth, covered the hole, and then I placed the flat stone on the grave.

I picked up my sword, returned it to my belt loop and walked home, making sure I didn't crush the skunk cabbage bending in silence to my left and to my right.

When Jesus Christ was born he taught us humility. He taught us to put away our foolish ways and follow him. It is difficult at times to recognize that our ambitions are nothing if they are selfish. Power gained without wisdom and love is evil power.

Take a look at your ambitions today. Ask yourself, do I seek advancement because I am following God's will, or Herod's?

All kings and queens, all emperors and presidents bow down to the Son of the carpenter, bless yourselves with the words from the Father almighty, maker of heaven and earth.

I pray that I may kiss the cheek of Christ so that I too may be king in the eyes of those I meet today.

Good Friday

Anyone who does not take his cross and follow me is not worthy of me.

MATTHEW 10:38

For me Good Friday means silence. When I was a child my mother and father insisted that, on this day, we children walk around the house quietly. No TV. No radio. No record player. We were asked not to play any games.

I remember sitting most of one particular Good Friday afternoon in my father's small office. He was a writer and spent many days in, what we called, the sun porch.

On that Good Friday I felt alone. I couldn't hear my sisters and brothers. The television was silent. My sister's record player wasn't echoing in the hallway.

I remember sitting on this large gray chair that unfolded into a bed. It was an uncomfortable chair: lumpy and full of springs. I began counting the pulled threads that were scattered on the back portion of the chair.

The next thing I knew it was completely dark. I had fallen asleep and woke up hours later with a blanket around me.

Obviously it was the middle of the night. The lights in the house were out. No one was downstairs. I was frightened, afraid to move from the chair or to call out for my father into the silence.

Each Good Friday I think about a little boy alone under his blanket with his cheeks pressed against the rough surface of an old chair.

I think about the darkness, and the silence, and the blanket my father had covered me with to protect me from the cold.

Christ endured the greatest silence and darkness on the Good Friday of long ago so that we, too, know where and how to carry our own cross. We are God's children who need the blanket of his dying on the cross for our salvation.

How do you carry your cross? Do you bathe your severely disabled child each morning, and watch the cool water run down his arms? Do you straighten out the crooked photograph of your mother who died many years ago? Do you feel the cool metal spoon on your tongue as you take your medication with confidence and joy that the new day is on display for you?

If you look closely at the routine of your suffering today, you will find your own powerful way of handling this burden.

Lord I found the straps that will help me adjust the daily burden of my pain. Lord I found the strength. I found, Lord, in my trial, the way to wisdom and salvation. You have left a clear path to follow. I found the mark in the ground where you dragged your cross.

Christ Looks Down Upon You

"Take courage! It is I. Don't be afraid."

MATTHEW 14:27

*D*o you fear the image of the Lord? I hope not. For as long as I can remember, the face of Christ looked down upon me.

One evening my father returned home from work with a heavy object wrapped under a brown blanket. It was a twelfth-century Russian portrait of Christ.

During his lunch break that afternoon, my father was walking through different antique shops in New York City when he found this artifact made of inlaid blue enamel. Christ's image was cast in bronze.

On the weekend my father mounted the bronze and enamel portrait on a piece of oak he had in the basement, and then he hung it above the fireplace.

The image of Christ looked down upon all the Christmas presents I received, listened to all the conversations I had with my family, and looked down upon all the hours I spent in the home of my childhood.

When my wife and I married, and we moved into our two bedroom home, I quietly drove on my own to a local art and frame shop. I ordered a reproduction of a twelfth-century portrait of Christ similar to the one my father bought. I brought the picture home a few weeks later, glued the poster onto a piece of oak, and covered the image with a thin layer of varnish; then I hung my picture in the house of my children yet to be born.

The image of Christ in my father's house is smiling. The image of Christ in my house is also smiling.

Today, as you enter your busy schedule, remember not to fear the Lord. He wants to be with you. He wants to look down on all that you do. He wants to hear your laughter.

I give thanks to the Lord for he is good (Ps 107:1). I give thanks to the Lord for he is happy. I give thanks to the Lord for he knows how to laugh.

Lending to the Lord

He who is kind to the poor lends to the Lord, and he will reward him for what he has done.

PROVERBS 19:17

Some years ago I was on my way home from a speech on my books in Syracuse, New York. My plane was due to depart at 8:15 in the evening. I arrived at the airport an hour before, checked in at the desk, bought a newspaper, and walked to gate twelve.

At each gate comfortable chairs sat before the large picture window. I like to watch the jets move before me like giant whales in a holding tank.

As I began to read the paper, I glanced around and noticed three or four people waiting for the incoming plane.

Great, I thought. Not many people. At least I'll have a peaceful flight home.

I continued reading the newspaper. Ten minutes later I was distracted once again and turned my head to my left. I looked over my shoulder and saw, down the long hall, a mob slowly walking toward me: fathers, mothers, children carrying balloons, teenagers carrying radios and Walkmans.

Keep walking, keep walking, I said to myself. There were over a hundred people, all going to Disney World, I thought. Keep walking.

I tried to seem unconcerned as I smoothed out my paper and began to read another article. I peered over the edge of the newspaper just as a red balloon floated by me. To my right an old, old woman sat down with a long sigh. Behind me a baby began to cry.

Within two minutes every seat, every space around me was filled with this tribe of nomads. Where are the camels? I laughed.

Were you ever caught in the middle of a drama?

I stood up and walked over to the courtesy desk and jokingly said to the woman, "Oh well. Here I thought I had the entire plane to myself."

"Oh, they're not flying. They're waiting for passengers from the incoming flight."

At first I didn't think to ask who was receiving such a welcoming committee, so I simply began walking among the people who were, indeed, waiting. Finally I couldn't contain my curiosity. I edged my way closer and closer to a circle of five people. "Excuse me, but I just can't help wondering. Who are you waiting for?"

"Oh," said the woman with a pleasant voice, "our church is sponsoring a family from Armenia. The father came three years ago. We've finally been able to bring over his wife, his children, and his grandparents. We're here to welcome them. The family hasn't been together for three years. This is their last stop. Their new home. They've been flying from Armenia, to Rome, to New York, and now, finally, here to Syracuse."

This was much better than the newspaper which I dumped into the trash can. Then I walked around a pillar among the large crowd as I tried to find a good spot to watch the reunion unfold.

Within ten minutes the large jet rolled out of the darkness. Its nose nearly touched the glass window. The crowd was visibly moved with the impending drama. People stood up, adjusted their cameras, untangled the balloons.

Armenia. Earthquakes. Genocide.

The door opened. Passengers, obviously not from Armenia and obviously surprised with the crowd in the hallway, quickly stepped through. As each new passenger emerged from the closed doors, the anxious crowd took closer and closer looks.

Finally, as the doors were held back, someone called out, "I see them! Here they come!"

I stood on a chair and stared beyond the heads of everyone in front of me. And there they were: three children wrapped in bright wool coats and scarves, a young woman in a long black coat with a purple scarf wrapped around her head, and an old, old man walking arm in arm with an old, old woman.

I will never forget how the church people cheered and brought the young man before the crowd. I will never forget how the wife broke away from her children and embraced her husband. The teenagers reached over to the three Armenian children and tried to hand them the red balloons. The smallest girl cried. The old grandfather broke out in a toothless grin that ought to be on the front cover of *Time* magazine.

The crowd cheered again and slowly walked together with the reunited family, down the carpeted hallway. Within minutes they were all gone, and all was as it was before.

Those who are kind to the poor are actually giving to the Lord. The Bible says God will reward them. After I witnessed the joy of this reunion, I wondered if God had not already rewarded everyone there.

Among our possessions, we can misplace the Lord. Lend to God today. Donate money or time to those that need it. You will be rewarded.

Lord of a thousand loaves and fish, may the coins in my hand jingle a song of hope as I share them with those who are in need. May the meal I prepare multiply as I feed those who are hungry. May the clothes I wear unfold to a multitude of clothes for those who are in need of warmth.

God of the Meek

Blessed are the meek, for they will inherit the earth.

MATTHEW 5:5

*A*lfred Lord Tennyson's poem "The Flower" contains the following lines:

I hold you here, root and all, in my hand
but if I could understand
what you are, root and all
I should know what God and man is.

Few people can understand those lines better than the parents of a retarded child.

In my house where I grew up, my mother and father spent thirty-two years holding the crippled, blind, mute, and brain-damaged body of my brother Oliver. He was "root and all" in their hands. They spent thirty-two years trying to understand him.

Do you know how many times a parent carries his mentally handicapped child from one place to another? Or leads him to the table? Or holds him during a convulsion?

My parents were forever lifting Oliver into the bathtub, carrying him outdoors to rest on a blanket in the sunlight, turning him back and forth in his bed.

Now suppose someone could incorporate the gesture of a mother holding her severely brain-damaged child as she soothes him in the middle of the night?

An entire national and international movement has been founded upon the simple gesture of the embrace. "I hold you here, root and all."

No organization I know of illustrates the power of the embrace better than the Special Olympics.

At a recent Special Olympic meet I attended, I heard a whistle. I turned my head to see five or six runners standing still, looking at the starter's gun.

Silence. Silence. *Bang!* The race was on.

Each child began to run. One Special Olympian immediately turned to the crowd and smiled; another threw his arms in all different directions like loose bits of rope. Then, with purpose, he ran into the far distance.

One girl ran with her feet pointed outward. Each athlete ran, walked, or slowly stepped with courage across the finish line where they were individually embraced by official "huggers": policemen, fathers, mothers, insurance brokers, lawyers, foremen, teenagers ... all volunteers. I watched the audience lean forward, willing each runner on with an invisible push.

At another event, a girl placed one foot onto the balance beam and then the other. This Special Olympian looked at her coach, asking with her eyes for assistance. Then she looked at the audience, waved and walked along the narrow wood, step by step, in her white socks.

Her legs shook. She turned slowly, crouching, slipped, regained her balance, stood up, turned toward the crowd, jumped off the beam and into the applause of every person in the stands.

What is behind the Special Olympics success? People publicly embracing the very root and stem of life, perhaps.

John, a Special Olympian from Glendale, Rhode Island said, "I like Special Olympics because it makes me feel good inside to be with other Special Olympians, to know everyone tried his best, and to know that everyone wins and loves one another."

I am startled at the God and man that is revealed to us again and again in the embrace of the Special Olympics.

Lord, I want to be of service to others. I want to help where there is a need for help. Bring to me today someone who is in need of an embrace. Teach me how to become an official hugger.

Simple Wonders

Stop and consider God's wonders.

JOB 37:14

I do not know anything about the habits of the ladybug. They seem to have the shell of a pea, their wings are red, and upon each wing a black dot sits in equal proportion to each other.

I used to believe ladybugs lived in dandelions.

I truly felt sorry for the ladybug who had to hurry home because her house was on fire, and once for my birthday someone gave me a ladybug brush to polish shoes.

My old friend Rosie on Mallison Street once explained that it was the ladybug that delivered babies and not storks. I read once that the ladybug could help a young girl find her lover. The girl places the insect on the tip of her fingers and instructs it to go home. When the ladybug flies off, the girl is to follow it to the place where the young man waits.

Find a ladybug on your dress and your mother will buy you a new one soon. According to folklore the ladybug announced the best time to begin the harvest and where the cattle have wandered.

A month ago, I discovered a ladybug sitting at the top of the south wall of the bathroom. It hasn't moved once. Each morning after my shower, I look up to check and see if it is still there upon the peach flowers of the wallpaper.

Is it still alive? Can a dead ladybug cling to the side of a wall for a month? I do not wish to disturb it. Do they hibernate? What does a ladybug eat? Aphids? There are no aphids in the bathroom.

I do not think about the ladybug throughout the day, but after my morning shower, I look up and there it is again. Does it look at me? Can it see? Of all the ladybugs that ever existed, why has this one found its way into the bathroom?

Superstition says that if you find a ladybug in the house in the winter, you will receive money soon.

Oracle of love, friend of the farmer, charmer of children in the yard. I like what we human beings have done with so many of the things that surround us. We give things names, create myths and stories about them, admire their colors. We are all scientists of a sort, observing what surrounds us.

There is a skylight in the bathroom and last night I noticed that the moon shines directly against the wall where the ladybug rests. When I strain my eyes in the darkness I see a vague spot on the wall.

No one else in the house has discovered my ladybug yet. She is my secret.

She is mine in the moonlight.

God created the universe! He created the stars! The heavens! He created the Grand Canyon! Niagara Falls! The Alps! All that is spectacular, God has created. But we can easily forget that God also created the single blade of grass, and the smallest piece of dust that floats in the sunlight of your room.

We should not forget that God is the Creator of all things great and small, even the ladybug.

Take a moment out of this day and see if you cannot recognize God's handiwork in the smallest thing: a single strand of your hair, or a drop of water on the window. If you look close enough, you will discover his thumbprint.

I do not see the world in the cup of a thimble. I do not see the world in the cup of the sea. Oh Lord, I see the world in the cup of your hands for they are vast and deep for all men and women to gather what has been created.

Godly People

Be rich in good deeds.

1 TIMOTHY 6:18

*I*f you want to be a good person, follow these simple rules:

1) Always give your baby-sitter a dollar more than she is expecting.
2) If your grandmother asks you to play cards with her, say yes.
3) Leave the last amount of orange juice in the refrigerator for your husband or wife.
4) When someone drives past you at night with his high beams blinding you, don't flash him in the eyes with your bright lights.
5) If your three-year-old child wants to crawl in bed with you at two in the morning, pull open your blanket and whisper "hop in."
6) Don't annoy your wife by refusing to touch the moon rock at the aviation museum in Washington, D.C.
7) After you finish driving your wife's car, be sure you readjust the seat so she can reach the foot pedals and the steering wheel.
8) Change the water in the fishbowl now.
9) Wash your hands after reading the newspaper.
10) If there is a wasp flying around your room, don't reach for the flyswatter; rather, reach over and open the window.

11) If someone asks you for advice on investing money, don't give it.

12) Turn the shower nozzle to the closed position when you are finished with your shower.

13) If you live within fifty yards of your neighbor's house, don't hang wind chimes on your back porch.

14) Do not hang wallpaper with your husband.

15) Do not hang wallpaper with your wife.

16) If the garbage can is full, take it out.

17) If you loan a book to someone, don't expect to get it back.

18) Let the neighborhood children play on your lawn.

19) If your five-year-old daughter asks for a piggyback ride down the stairs, give it to her.

20) Let your wife pay the bills.

21) Refill the paper tray of the copy machine when you are finished.

22) When you are at the zoo, don't feed the animals.

The apostle Paul explained to Timothy to instruct the church people who followed him "to do good, to be rich in good deeds, and to be generous and willing to share" (1 Tm 6:18). In this way, said Paul, they will lay up treasures for themselves and for their children.

There are twenty-two examples above. What deeds will you be able to add to the list just before you go to bed tonight?

I do not wish to serve my boss. I do not wish to serve my time schedule. I do not wish to serve money. All that I do, I do for the Lord. All that I serve, I serve in the name of the Lord.

To Dream, To Imagine,
To Dream Again

Now to him who is able to do immeasurably more than all we ask or imagine, according to his power that is at work within us, to him be glory in the church and in Christ Jesus throughout all generations, for ever and ever! Amen.

EPHESIANS 3:20-21

There was a box. I do not remember how this box appeared in my life. We accumulate objects that are created by human hands. No one can predict the nature of a child's fancy. He will love a crooked stick from the yard as much as he will be enchanted with a steel and iron electric engine huffing and puffing along the gray tracks on the living room floor.

My box was in the shape of a rectangle about two feet wide and one foot high. It was the right size for a boy to carry from room to room, the right size to store metal cars with rubber wheels and fake rings with glass emeralds extracted from the little machines shaped like bubbles which sat upon metal posts waiting for little boys at the door of the food store.

I kept this box made from wood under my bed within reach at anytime, the best time just before going to sleep. I kept my Superman comic books, a tobacco pipe I found in the garage, puries (clear, colored marbles, the rarest in our neighborhood), a trick hand-buzzer, an Indian head penny, a candle, my ice-cream stick collection (good for weaving into small rafts for the lake each summer). All these baubles were kept safe inside my box.

But something more, which is usually the case with little boys. Always something more beyond what they expected. This box had a feature I didn't pay much attention to at first. Now that I look back, I realize I never understood how much the colorful illustration meant to me.

Open the box and I will show you my candles and marbles, and more. Now I will show you the picture pasted inside, behind the top, a picture of a tall ship tied to a pier. This ship belonged to a distant time when the wind blew commerce from sea to sea in the pocket of giant sails held together with thick ropes tied to solid masts.

Look closely. Step down. See the colors of the sky? I like the blue and how the reflection of the ship is seen in the water, a crooked image. Perhaps the captain is sitting behind his door. If you look closely, there is a yellow light beyond the small window.

Can you feel the deck? Is it moist under your fingers? Here, gently touch the wood. I pretend my finger is a man invited for a grand tour. I usually start from the left and walk slowly to the right until the cook steps out from behind this door and hands me an orange. Once I imagined a seagull, and turned the robin's cry in the yard into a seagull cry.

It is best to stretch on your back and place the box on your stomach. (It is easier to pretend in this position.) With my head on the pillow I like to gently rock the box back and forth and measure the strength of my ship against the storm rising. I can see—really see— the waves crashing against the hull. There is a small boy hiding in the empty pickle barrel as the wind howls. The captain shouts an order to lower the sails. See? And I am afraid, though I don't admit it as a whale—one can always count on a whale—leaps just beyond the tall ship and harpoons and mermaids and light and rain and thunder.

"Chrissy! Dinner!"

I slam the lid shut—bang!—slide the box back under my bed, roll onto the carpet, stand, wobble with my sea legs (my older brother told me about sea legs).

There was a box which held the first lessons on how to imagine beyond my bedroom walls. I haven't sailed upon a better ship, or found a more suitable pickle barrel.

We are the only creatures of God born with an imagination. We can fly, breathe under water, and create music like Mozart in our imagination.

Imagine, today, what it will be like to someday sit beside God and share a pot of tea with him.

For the power to dream, I thank you Lord. For the power to create, I praise you. For the gift of the imagination, I thank you Lord. For the gladness in my heart, I praise you.

We Are Created By God

It is good for us to be here.

MATTHEW 17:4

Our cat is like a lion, a creature of paradise stretched out on the floral print rug yawning in satisfaction. Mittens was born in a barn and destined to live a barnyard life, fending for herself, eating field mice, receiving an occasional bowl of warm milk from the routinely milked cows that have spent the day eating grass.

I announced one afternoon to my students in the rural high school where I taught that my children wished for a cat, an orange cat. I asked the young men and women, "Has anyone got a kitten they're anxious to place?" You would think I asked if anyone had warts they'd like eradicated. Every student, it seemed, had a cat, a kitten, ten kittens, any kitten, every kitten to give away happily. Some even said the cats would come with a bag of litter.

I drove to three farms in my quest for a possible creature to adopt. I saw black cats the size of the king's panther. I saw thin, gray cats that could fit between a mail slot. There were calico cats, fat cats, silly cats, sleeping cats. No orange cat.

The selection of a cat depends more on irrational requirements than on sound judgment. "Orange, Daddy. The kitten has to be orange." My daughter explained each time I returned home without a cat.

Orange. Orange. Perhaps I could take a few lessons from Lewis

Carroll as the frightened deck of cards painted the discolored roses red to satisfy the queen.

I had two little barons and a little baroness to satisfy at home. Orange kitten. "You wouldn't want a brown one, or a gold one? Gold, that's close to orange," I asked my children before driving to school one morning. I remembered their answer as I drove up to the fourth farm that afternoon. "Orange, Daddy. We'd like an orange cat."

As I stepped out from my car in the driveway, a man, obviously the farmer, walked out of his barn.

"Hello. I'm Chris de Vinck, one of the teachers from the high school. Your son said in class this morning that you have kittens you'd like to find homes for?"

"You want them all?" the father asked.

I looked toward the barn with its yawning door. Cats and kittens tumbled, rolled, ran, stalked out from the door as if they were in a grand parade. Then, as if on cue, out pranced the picture my daughter tore out of a magazine. An orange kitten.

"What about that one?" I asked the farmer.

"Take them all, if you'd like."

As I drove home, the kitten didn't cry once, rather it stood on the right seat and watched the trees pass overhead. She looked at me several times wondering, perhaps, what type of strange barn I was.

When I arrived home, the children greeted me in the driveway. I lifted the kitten out of the car and handed it to six reaching hands.

"Look! It's orange!"

"Is it a boy or a girl?"

"Can I sleep with it?"

"It's a girl," I said.

"It has white paws."

"Let's name her Mittens!"

So Mittens it was.

Stretched out on the smooth plains of the living room carpet an orange cat sleeps on its back with its paws in various positions, and its head turned to a comfortable position. The children are sleeping. I can see small red flowers in the carpet's design. Yellow flowers. Green and blue. Mittens opened her eyes, blinked once, and returned to her dream of haystacks and field mice.

In Genesis 1:24-25 it is written that "God said 'Let the land produce living creatures according to their kinds: livestock, creatures that move along the ground, and wild animals, each according to its kind.' And it was so. God made the wild animals according to their kinds, the livestock according to their kinds, and all the creatures that move along the ground according to their kinds. And God saw that it was good."

God created the animals in the world for our joy. It is easy to take for granted a single sparrow jumping back and forth in the bushes. Can you imagine a world without any animals at all: no whales, no crickets, no geese, no squirrels, no armadillo, no orange kittens?

"It is good for us to be here," St. Matthew wrote. The very first animal you see today look at it as if you are seeing it for the first time. Take great delight in what you see. Take great delight in its Creator.

Dear God, you created me in your own image. Am I the image of the Lord, the face of your love? I pray that I take delight today in all you have created, for there is no greater work than the work from your hands. It is good to be in your house.

Missing God's Blessing

Sons are a heritage from the Lord, children a reward from him.
Like arrows in the hands of a warrior are sons born in one's youth.
Blessed is the man whose quiver is full of them.

PSALM 127:3-5

I had finally had it. The children were loud, cranky, impossible. I was tired and fed up. My wife was tired and fed up. I decided that I was going to run away from it all and have a day just for me. I wanted to spoil myself. I wanted to have a day where I did just what I wanted to do. I was going to live it up and be as greedy as I pleased. I wasn't going to tend to anyone except myself.

I zoomed out of the house with fifty dollars. There! I did it, I said to myself as I drove to the highway and headed north.

Well, I drove to a mall and had a wild time in a bookstore and bought the collected poems of Walt Whitman. After that I drove and drove to a McDonalds and ordered *two* hamburgers, my *own* large fries, and my *own* large soda. I ate everything *without* being interrupted, without giving my pickle to *anyone*, without wiping someone's mouth, nose, lap. Then I bought the *biggest* chocolate ice-cream cone I could find.

I was free. I was out on the town, so I drove to a movie theater and watched a movie without buying popcorn, without someone sitting on my lap, without escorting someone to the bathroom. I was a free man. I was living it up. And I was miserable.

By the time I had returned home, everyone was asleep. As I

slipped into bed, my wife whispered, "We missed you." "Me too," I answered. I never ran away from home again.

If you are in the middle of the pressures of raising a family, remember, it's no fun being alone.

"Children are a reward from the Lord," writes the psalmist. So take the kids today to McDonalds, or to a bookstore, or to the movies. Take them anywhere except out of your heart.

Lonely in my heart, Lord. Lonely in my heart. I am not lonely in my heart because of the children on the swing, the children under the blankets, because of the children in the house, the house of the Lord, my Lord you who have blessed me with the children, Lord, the children. I am not lonely. Amen I say to you with gratitude for the children. For this I pray.

Encouragement That
Goes On and On

May our Lord Jesus Christ ... encourage your hearts and strengthen you in every good deed and word.

2 THESSALONIANS 2:16-17

*M*any years ago, after I decided to write a column for newspapers on a weekly basis, I sent out a number of letters to different editors wondering if they would be interested in my work. I sent them copies of articles I had printed in national journals, and excerpts from my books. After a few weeks I was invited to submit my columns to ten newspapers across the country.

The very first column appeared in a newspaper in Albany, New York. From that point, my essays appeared regularly. After a few weeks passed, my first reader's response was printed in the newspaper's letter section.

It was a splendid review. A reader said how impressed she was with the writing, with the perceptions, with the depth of understanding that my columns exhibited. The letter was signed C. Kesten.

On the afternoon the review arrived in my mailbox, my wife was shopping. When she returned I said, "Roe, look at this first response from one of my new readers!" I was excited that *someone* liked what I was writing.

Roe sat at the kitchen table, read the letter in the newspaper, turned up to me and smiled. I smiled. Then she started to laugh.

"Chris! Your mother wrote that!"

"My mother. How do you know?"

"C. Kesten. Who do you think that is?"

"My mother's maiden name was Kestens, with an S at the end. You know that."

"Well," Roe said with another smile, "sounds like your mother to me."

I phoned my mother right away. "I couldn't resist," she said with a wonderful voice of joy and humor.

So my very first review of praise about my writing came from my mother. I've won awards for my writing, given many talks about writing, had books published since, but no review will ever top the one from my mother in that Albany newspaper of many years ago.

Encouragement. It lasts for a day. For a day. For a lifetime. "May our Lord Jesus Christ himself and God our Father, who loved us and by his grace gave us eternal encouragement and good hope, encourage your hearts and strengthen you in every good deed and word" (2 Thes 2:16-17).

As you think about all the encouragement God has given to you in your lifetime so far, perhaps you can think of someone who could use a simple word of encouragement from you today. Is someone about to make a presentation? Is someone going to be taking a test? Is someone you know going on a job interview?

We all take risks at times for the betterment of ourselves and those around us. Like Christ in the Garden of Gethsemane, we also all need human and divine encouragement to be who we were sent to be upon this good earth.

Lord God in my race against evil, as I weave around selfishness, as I run past anger, as I begin to lose energy around the track of my life, I clearly hear you applauding for me in the audience which gives me the courage to complete my race in victory. For this I am thankful.

The Hope of God

*And hope does not disappoint us, because God has poured out his
love into our hearts by the Holy Spirit, whom he has given us.*

ROMANS 5:5

My nine-year-old son Michael requested stars for his birthday. He asked for an entire universe: shooting stars, constellations. "You can throw in Saturn and the moon too."

I asked Michael how he thought up the idea of hoping for the
universe for his birthday.

"I don't want the universe. I just want stars on my ceiling.
Remember at that store."

I had forgotten.

"You remember, Daddy. The store where we saw the dinosaur
coloring book and the telescopes? Remember? There were these
long, hollow sticks from Africa with beans inside. Remember when
we turned the stick upside down it sounded like there was a water-
fall in the stick?"

I remembered.

"On a shelf I found stars in a plastic bag. You can stick them on
the ceiling. They glow in the dark. Stars. That's what I'd like for my
birthday."

Did you ever wish for something extraordinary? A fancy house?
A new car? Lots of property? Perfect health? A child? A husband
or wife? Peace of mind? Michael said the other day that he is sav-
ing his allowance.

"What for?" I asked.

"A dolphin. When I have enough money I'm going to build a huge pool and buy a dolphin."

How can we control our imagination? How can we match what we hope for with what we have?

What are your plans for the day? A walk? A busy schedule at work? Tending to the children? Do you look out the window sometimes and just imagine how things could be different, or better, or easier?

After Michael's birthday party, at the end of the day, he and I walked to his room. We opened the plastic bag and stuck over fifty illuminating stars to his ceiling.

"If you hold the lamp close to them, they'll glow better," Michael suggested.

That is what I did. As I held his lamp in my right hand, I looked like the Statue of Liberty. When Michael and I decided that the stars had been exposed to the light long enough, I placed the lamp on the table beside his bed.

"Let's lie on our backs on the bed and pretend we're outside looking at the stars," Michael said.

I clicked off the lamp. "Hey! Look!" Michael nearly laughed with satisfaction. "They really look like stars!"

We admired the glowing lights on the ceiling. I pressed my hand behind my head. Michael did the same. We two were astronomers, discovering new constellations. Who is to say that Michael and I did not capture the universe in his small room that night: a boy and his father with their hands behind their heads looking up to what they both knew was wonderful.

We do not have to pretend that we have attained joy and comfort. We do not have to spend the day feeling, somehow, that we haven't attained our goals.

Instead of a dolphin, Michael bought a goldfish and a goldfish bowl with his allowance. Best looking dolphin I've ever seen.

Today, as you think about what you hope for the most, look around and take notice: you probably already have what is good and holy and simple—the true stars of the universe and the true dolphins swimming above and around your heart.

It is the same with our hope in God: it never disappoints. We can hope for certain things, and if it is God's will, those things will come to pass, but if we hope for God his entrance into our lives is an absolute certainty.

Tonight take a close look at the stars that God and his Son stuck to the ceiling of the universe and be glad.

God of the stars, God of my dreams, I build the house of my life upon your foundation: faith, hope, and love. Let us pray that all who build subscribe to the same architect—you, my Lord and Savior.

Isn't Life Good?

For I am convinced that neither death nor life ... nor anything else in all creation, will be able to separate us from the love of God that is in Christ Jesus our Lord.

ROMANS 8:38-39

When my father was a college professor a young student from China, a Mr. Tong, enrolled in his class. After a few months, my father learned that Mr. Tong was married, had three small children, and was thousands of miles from home.

My father invited this young man to our house for many weekends. Each time he came, Mr. Tong would become more and more at ease with my family.

We all learned that he planned to earn his degree in economics and then return to China to be reunited with his family. Unfortunately, the government of China endured a great upheaval, and Mr. Tong could not return to his country. For twenty-five years Mr. Tong wrote to his family. Eventually, the Chinese government endured, again, another upheaval and Mr. Tong was able to bring his wife and children to the United States.

For all those lonely years, Mr. Tong remained faithful to his wife. When he was reunited with her, he later said that they had to become reacquainted all over again for it was almost as if they were strangers.

Today all of Mr. Tong's children are graduates of the best universities in this country. Mr. Tong is a grandfather many times over.

He still visits my parents. "Isn't life good," he will say often.

Remember the famous words: To have and to hold from this day forward, for better for worse, for richer for poorer, in sickness and in health, to love and to cherish, till death us do part.

Mr. Tong was able to cherish. He was able to hold on to his love for his wife for all the years they were apart. God's love is able to hold on to us his bride, the church, in spite of any difficulties, too. "For I am convinced that neither death nor life, neither angels nor demons, neither the present nor the future, nor any powers, neither height nor depth, nor anything else in all creation, will be able to separate us from the love of God that is in Christ Jesus our Lord" (Rom 8:38-39).

If there is a small break between you and someone you love, think of Mr. Tong, and try and patch things up today. And if it seems that there is a break between you and God, remember, the Bible says that such a break is not possible.

"Isn't life good?"

Sweet Lord, have patience with us. We build walls that divide. We close doors to keep others out. Teach us how to topple the walls stone by stone. Show us how to open the doors and bless all who enter.

He Restores My Soul

He makes me lie down in green pastures, he leads me beside quiet waters, he restores my soul.

PSALM 23:2-3

In the first year of our marriage, Roe and I bought an antique regulator clock. It will run for seven days with a full winding of the spring. During the first week, after we hung the clock on the wall, I couldn't sleep well. I dislike the sound of ticking. It drums into my head. I count each tick-tock. There was no use.

For two years, each time we were ready to walk up the stairs for the night, I stopped the clock's pendulum. In the morning, I'd reset the clock, push the pendulum, and the ticking would continue again throughout the day, until the moments before Roe and I went to bed.

Into the third year of our marriage, I stopped winding the clock altogether, not bothering to stop and restart the thing any longer.

For the past thirteen years the clock has remained silent on the wall in the family room. I like silence when I sleep. We have an electric clock. Water doesn't drip in the bathroom. Silence is a luxury.

My friends and my children often ask why I don't get my clock fixed. I say again and again that it is working just fine.

We have to sometimes arrange our lives according to our own needs. It is good to be generous, giving, loving, but it is also good to, every now and then, treat ourselves.

Jesus set this example, for himself and for those who followed

133

him. In the middle of the press and crush of need, he turned his disciples' attention toward their own concerns. "Because so many people were coming and going that they did not even have a chance to eat, he said to them, 'Come with me by yourselves to a quiet place and get some rest'" (Mk 6:31).

Today might be a good day to rearrange something in your life that will bring you a little comfort and peace.

The sun keeps me warm, and the evening mist of summer keeps me cool. When I am hungry bread and fish keep me from hunger. But no sun, no wind, no food has brought me as much warmth, fresh air, and comfort as your love for me Lord God of the sun, God of the air, God of the smallest grain of rice.

In the Image of God

So God created man in his own image, in the image of God he created him; male and female he created them.

GENESIS 1:27

What habits do you cherish? Do you like to sit before the mirror in the evening and unpin your hair? Do you brush your hair a certain number of times? When you look in the mirror, do you think about the changing face that you see? Do you remember when you were young? Do you remember when you stood before the mirror and feared that you might not be pretty? Do you remember looking deep into the image that looked back at you and you wondered if what you saw was real?

My mother had a long mirror in her bedroom. I nearly believed that I could walk through this mirror and join Alice and the White Rabbit and the Mad Hatter.

I remember watching my mother adjust her hair with pins and combs. My mother kept in a dresser her long, blonde curls that were cut when she was a teenager.

I watch Roe dry her hair each morning. I watch as she brushes her wet hair. I watch as she rubs her dark hair with a towel until her day-image appears.

Beauty is the product of the eye and heart. Without an image there is nothing. Without love there is nothing. Self love begins with a close look in the mirror and an acceptance that what we see is beautiful and good. After such an experience, what remains dur-

135

ing the day is beautiful and good.

The belief in God's unconditional approval of who we are and what we look like comes from knowing what God says about us, his extraordinary creative act: "I praise you [God] because I am fearfully and wonderfully made; your works are wonderful, I know that full well" (Ps 139:14).

At night, before you sleep, brush your hair, feel the texture, remember the hands that caressed it: a mother, a child perhaps, a husband. Place the brush and comb down gently on the dresser and lie in bed. Rest your head on the pillow and dream about the mirror, the image maker, for it reflects the sculpture, you, that God has created.

Lord God, Creator of things seen and unseen, I am the clay between your hands, the stone at the tip of your chisel. I am the artist's masterpiece for you are the master and I your creation. Let no one criticize your work. I am wonderfully made.

Paradise

In the middle of the garden [was] the tree of life.

GENESIS 2:9

In the house where I grew up there was a large oak table in the living room. This was the table that was once in a great chateau in Belgium where my father grew up. When he immigrated to this country with my mother in 1948, among the items he brought over the ocean was this table.

For as long as I can remember this table stood in the living room. I know it has been in the same spot for over forty-five years.

The only radio in the house sat on this table. I used to listen to cowboy songs on Saturday afternoon from that green radio. I'd sprawl myself on the tabletop, adjust the radio dial, and listen to a distant voice accompanied by a jumping guitar tune.

This table was the table my father used when he wrote many of his books. I remember hundreds of typed papers scattered about on the hard surface. I remember my father leaning over these papers as if he was weeding the garden with great care.

There was something else about the living room table that pleased me when I was a child. The legs were large, round, and connected to each other with a thick, wide band of solid oak that had fancy grooves in the entire length. These grooves were perfect for rolling marbles. I remember placing the marbles in a row in these grooves and pushing them along, as I pretended the marbles were train cars bumping into each other.

Perhaps it is not true that I spent hours at a time under the table pushing the marbles back and forth along those thin grooves in the wood, but in today's memory it seems like hours. I sometimes wish that I could return to the table and push the marbles while my mother and father read aloud, or my brother played a song on the piano, or my sister quietly painted on a paper bag in the kitchen.

Paradise is a memory away, just within our grasp. Reach out and it will become what is real.

I would like to return to my childhood and relive what it felt like to hold glass marbles in my hand while stew cooked in the kitchen pot and my mother called us in to wash our hands, and my father pulled off his glasses and placed them on top of his papers that covered the table. I liked the times when we were all together, my sisters, my brothers and I. I like to think of these times when I am tired. Perhaps that is what God has in store for us: a place where we are all together with the Father as we rush to dinner where the sounds of his house are full of delight.

Think about the first Tree of Life that is written about in the Book of Genesis. And think about the last Tree of Life written about in the Bible's last book: "To him who overcomes, I will give the right to eat from the tree of life, which is in the paradise of God" (Rv 2:7).

In addition to my memories that God will return to me again in paradise, I take delight in knowing he will give me the Tree of Life.

I remember my father's horn-rimmed glasses. I remember the place of my childhood. I believe heaven is full of smells of fresh stew, and the voice of my mother calling us in for the evening meal.

I can still hear the glass marbles ticking and clicking against themselves as they rattle along the grooves of the hard wood. I think God has those glass marbles waiting for me.

Today remember some of your happiest memories, for then you will have a glimpse of paradise.

Lord God I remember my home, for my home was a place of comfort and peace. Now I am on my way to your house. I have read your invitation in the Bible. I received your invitation delivered to my heart. I am coming. Please guide me so that I do not lose my way.

Lord of the Brokenhearted
and the Bitter

[The Lord] heals the brokenhearted and binds up their wounds.

PSALM 147:3

Open wounds are the source of constant pain. A pine tree bleeds sap. The sun divides the night from the day that causes a constant division between light and darkness.

I knew a man, an only child, who believed that his father cheated him out of an inheritance. The father belonged to a local charity organization. Each year the father's group raised money to send an ill child to a place of his or her dream: Disney World, perhaps, or the dugout of the New York Yankees, or perhaps to a grandmother's house on the other side of the world.

When the father died he donated all he had to this organization. The son tried to recover the money through the courts, but the suit was settled in favor of the charity group.

For a long time the son complained about the world's injustice. He often cursed the name of his father.

Five years after the death of the father, the son contracted a heart ailment and was rushed to the hospital. It was determined that the son needed a triple bypass. The son died. In his will it was discovered that he too donated all he owned to the same charitable organization as his father had.

Even though the son lived with bitterness for five years, he claimed a final victory for himself by his act of generosity. But think what the son's last five years could have been like if he had let in the Lord who heals the brokenhearted.

Is there a wound in your life that you have been nursing, or a grudge you won't allow to heal? Perhaps you can, today, think about how you can heal your bitterness. Pray to God. Ask him how your brokenheartedness could end. He will give you an answer.

I can see the failures, Lord, in the deeds of others. I can be quick to identify bitterness. Help me accept failure in those that I love and in my own life. Help me turn my own anger into a reconciliation for there is no greater compromise than the compromise of the heart. You are my ambassador. Help me deliver true words and deeds of reconciliation to those who are bitter.

Pray for God's Peace

Then the land had rest from war.

JOSHUA 11:23

Each time I visit Washington, D.C., either for pleasure with my family or for business in my career in education and writing, I visit the Smithsonian Institute because I want to touch the black-and-white checkered rocket.

When I was a child my father told me the story of the V-2 rockets, how they would fly over from the enemy's borders and explode in Belgium. "If you could still hear the engine of the rocket, that meant it was still flying and you had nothing to worry about, but if the engine stopped, that meant the rocket was falling to the ground." The V-2 rockets were flying bombs. They destroyed many homes in Belgium and killed many people.

When I visit the Washington museum, I stroke the sides of one of these bombs of destruction and pray for the families who lost those they loved because of such ugliness. Then I thank God for the long-ago safety of my father.

My father is eighty-two years old. He likes to cut and fold paper airplanes for his grandchildren. My children will never know the sounds of bombs falling upon them, and my father is still able to laugh.

God wants us to love each other. What torment it must be for him to see people killing people. War is the evidence of chaos, evidence of evil, evidence of the devil's work.

Neighborhood strife or international world wars. There is no difference. If we pray, we and God will be the victors. "He will judge between the nations and will settle disputes for many peoples. They will beat their swords into plowshares and their spears into pruning hooks. Nation will not take up sword against nation, nor will they train for war anymore. Come, O house of Jacob, let us walk in the light of the Lord" (Is 2:4-5).

Today is a good day to walk in the light of the Lord. Think of those who have died so that others may live in freedom and in peace.

Lord, I pray for peace in my heart, and for peace in my house. I pray, Lord, for peace in my neighborhood, and for peace in my state. I pray for peace in my country, for peace in my world. I pray, Lord God, for such peace for today and for all eternity.

The God Who Gives

Until now you have not asked for anything in my name. Ask and you will receive, and your joy will be complete.

JOHN 16:24

*T*his past October I taught, perhaps, the last class I will ever teach. I have been a teacher for sixteen years, and now I am a school administrator. The new job means a shorter commute, and a new challenge. As I looked back to all that I did in the classroom, I became frightened of my new position. How do I start something new all over again? Did I make a mistake leaving the classroom?

How do you deal with serious decisions you need to make? I share my concerns with my family. I look to people I admire and see what they did with their lives, but then I still have to make the decision on my own.

I have always depended on that deep-inside voice to guide me in my life. That voice didn't fail me when I hoped to meet my someday wife. That voice didn't fail me when I sought strength as I tried to teach, write, be a husband and father. That voice didn't fail me when I hoped my writing would grow.

Someone once said to me that we should ask God for big gifts and graces. We shouldn't be afraid. We aren't greedy people. We know what God likes to hear. We know he likes us to ask for help, and he *always* does.

I tell my three children that I cannot solve all their problems, but

I can always help them with any difficult situation they encounter along the way.

Change is frightening, but I go home to the same wife, the same children, and to the same cat. They are still there, and I pray to the same God. He's still there too.

Have you asked God for anything lately? Have you asked him for something extraordinary? He will not help you win the lottery. He will not help you discover the fountain of youth. You and God both know exactly what things you can ask for. What is the biggest thing missing in your heart? Ask God to help you find that missing part. That deep, personal need is greater than gold. God provides. You just have to ask.

I have been afraid, Lord, to ask you for help. I sometimes believe you are too busy to be concerned with my small needs. Hear me, Father. I come to you in obedience for you have said ask and I shall receive. I ask, Lord, for your blessing. I ask for your help. Provide, provide, Lord God you provide.

Heaven's Gate

For by him all things were created: things in heaven and on earth, visible and invisible.

COLOSSIANS 1:16

Some time ago a crow discovered the rabbit's nest that was carefully hidden in the periwinkle. As Roe and the children and I were sitting in the family room, we heard a loud squeal. As we looked through the window we saw the crow flip a two-week-old rabbit out of the nest and onto the grass. The children, my wife, and I gave a loud scream as we rushed outside and chased the crow away.

The rabbit died. Five-year-old Karen wanted to help me bury the creature. She grabbed her blue plastic sandbox shovel. I pulled the spade out from the garage.

After we quickly dug a grave under the rhododendron, I placed the rabbit in a paper towel.

"Can I put him in the hole?" Karen asked.

"Of course you can."

Karen and I stooped down. Just as she was about to place the rabbit into the open ground, she turned up to me and asked, "Can I kiss him first?"

"Of course you can kiss him." And Karen kissed the paper towel which contained the lifeless shape; then she lowered her hand into the hole and placed the rabbit among the roots and moist earth.

"Is he thirsty now?" Karen asked.

"What's that, Karen?"

"When you die, are you thirsty?"

"Sure. And there's plenty to drink in heaven."

We covered the rabbit with the dark soil. I was about to place a large flagstone over the grave, but Karen didn't like that. She couldn't tell me why, but she did want to place a cross made of two twigs over the grave. This is what we did.

As we walked back into the house, Karen's small hand felt warm and strong in mine.

I will leave fancy theories of life and death to the scientists, and I will leave myth-making to ancient people. Karen and I solved the problem in a single afternoon: rabbits drink in heaven.

Children need to be told of God's promise of salvation. Children need to know from the voice of those they love that Christ will be beside them all their lives, easing their journey toward God's eternal embrace.

In a way you are also a child, a child of Christ. Listen as he tells you of his promise. Feel his presence beside you as you walk through your day.

Think today about who will lead you toward God's embrace: the Lord, Jesus Christ, your guide, your Father. Believe in him and all things shall be reconciled in eternal happiness.

You have eased my way, oh Lord, you have eased my way to heaven with your love and promise. You have eased my way to salvation. Alleluia, alleluia. You have eased my way.

The God of All Comfort

As a mother comforts her child, so will I comfort you.

ISAIAH 66:13

Someone told me the other night about a Tolstoy story called "The Lament." It is a simple story about an old man who drives a horse and buggy through the city for hire.

The story goes that the old man's son died recently and he wants so desperately to tell someone.

A wealthy man hires the horse and buggy for a ride across town. As the wealthy man steps into the carriage, the old man says, "My son, my son. Let me tell you about my son." But the busy man doesn't have time to listen.

Well after the wealthy man leaves, another man steps into the carriage. He wants to be driven to the other side of the city. Again, the old man says, "My son. My son. Let me tell you about my son." And again, this second man also doesn't bother to listen.

At the end of the day, the old man returns to the stables, unhitches his horse, and as he begins to brush the horse down for the night, the old man begins to tell the horse, "My son. My son." And he tells the horse the tragic story.

Isn't it wonderful that you are never alone, especially when you need comfort during your difficult times. "Praise be to the God and Father of our Lord Jesus Christ, the Father of compassion and the God of all comfort, who comforts us in all our troubles, so that we can comfort those in any trouble with the comfort we ourselves have received from God" (2 Cor 1:3-4).

We need to speak about our grief. We need to release our sorrow. This old, simple man in the story knew he had something important to say. We are all poets. We all have extraordinary things to say about very ordinary, but very important things in our lives.

Are you keeping something bottled up inside of you this morning? Share your grief with someone. It will make a difference. Or make yourself available to someone today who has recently been given a new burden of sadness. You have the ability to comfort and be comforted.

The substance of my sorrow is the substance of my peace. Help me Father in heaven to turn a neighbor's grief to a newfound wisdom: you, God of comfort, God of the embrace. Teach me how to soothe as you have soothed me.

A Clue to Happiness

"How can this be?"

When I was a child my mother told me the story about the doorbell.

"Christopher, when I was a little girl in Belgium there was a wealthy woman who lived down the street.

"This woman," my mother continued, "had fancy oil lamps, maids, and a cook. One day there was a rumor in the neighborhood: 'The rich lady, she's got a bell in her door.'"

My mother explained to me that this rich woman was the first person on her street to have an electric doorbell installed in her house. I remember my mother saying that all the children ran to the house, *knocked* on the woman's door and asked permission to ring her bell.

"Well," my mother said, "we rang that bell all afternoon, it seems to me."

I was reminded of my mother's story this afternoon as I listened to Nikolari Rimsky-Korsakov's "Procession of the Nobles."

I sat at my desk with my eyes closed and listened to the music when suddenly I heard a distant voice.

"What are you doing, Daddy?" Karen, my seven-year-old daughter asked as she entered the room.

"I'm listening to wonderful music."

"It sounds like kings dancing," Karen said as she sat on my lap.

As the recording ended, she asked, "Can we listen to it again?"

We sat together, my daughter and I, for nearly an hour listening to the same piece of music over and over again. That is a clue to happiness. When you come across something wonderful, like the sound of a doorbell, or a beautiful symphony, stick with it, surround yourself with the beauty you discovered. Share the beauty again and again with those you love.

I carried my daughter in my arms up to her bedroom where, after a prayer and a small kiss, she quietly slept.

"Be happy ... while you are young, and let your heart give you joy in the days of your youth. Follow the ways of your heart and whatever your eyes see" (Eccl 11:9). You can maintain your youth by seeing things as children see them: with delight. Be happy. It is God's will.

"Rejoice in the Lord always. I will say it again: Rejoice! Let your gentleness be evident to all" (Phil 4:4-5).

The more you surround yourself with beauty, the more beauty you will see. The more you rejoice in the Lord, the closer he will be to your heart. Today, rejoice!

To you I sing. To you I dance. To you I lift up my arms in honor and delight. Come to me in my singing. Come to me in my dance. Come to me, Lord Jesus. The celebration is at hand.

Little Children and the Kingdom of Heaven

"I tell you the truth, unless you change and become like little children, you will never enter the kingdom of heaven."

MATTHEW 18:3

Mrs. Robbins had a flat basket attached to her front door, a brown basket in the shape of a pouch, a large pocket, a place for notes, I figured. Mrs. Robbins also had a bell to the right of her door, a bell with a string. Standing before Mrs. Robbins' door was a small adventure for a boy of eight.

"Do I pull the bell, or write her a note?" I didn't have important things to say when I was eight. I remember posting Mrs. Robbins acorns in her mail basket, and ringing her bell just to say hello. She always answered the door with a loud, pleasing southern accent. "Hello Christopher."

It was rumored that Mrs. Robbins' grandfather was once a wealthy landowner in Tennessee.

"What can I do for you today?"

Mrs. Robbins was one of the few adults in my childhood memory who treated me like an adult. I'd hook my thumb in my pants pocket, stand tall and say, "Hello, Mrs. Robbins." Then I'd stand there not wanting to admit I mailed her acorns, or that I just liked ringing her front bell.

She'd walk out of the house and sit down on her stoop. I'd sit beside her and she'd tell me about the possum she found in her garbage can that morning, or about the cookies she was baking in the kitchen. When you are eight it is difficult to decide which is the better topic: possums or cookies.

I'd dig the heel of my right shoe in the dirt, or scratch a scab on my arm as I too explained important things to Mrs. Robbins: the color of my bedroom, or the arrival date of my grandparents from Belgium.

"Would you like to come inside for a while and have cookies and milk with me?" Mrs. Robbins would ask. "Ginger cookies?"

I always knew they'd be ginger cookies, usually in the shape of animals.

"Sure!"

Possums, grandparents, acorns, baskets. Let us not ignore the children who walk into our lives. Let us not forget the taste of ginger cookies.

Mrs. Robbins acted like Jesus. He is full of enthusiasm for simple things, full of delight when a child sits beside him, full of an inner peace that affects all who meet him. Jesus wouldn't shoo away a child knocking at his door. "Whoever welcomes a little child like this in my name welcomes me" (Mt 18:5).

Today take delight in the children. Share their enthusiasm for little things. Call your grandson on the phone and invite him to a slumber party at your house this weekend. Pick up your daughter after school today and take her out for an ice-cream cone. Be like Christ and welcome the children.

Dear Lord, thank you for my memories of my childhood. Thank you for letting me be childlike and not childish. I am who I was as a child. I am who I am today: man-child, woman-child. How good it is to be human. How good it is to be welcomed by you when I stand at your door and ring the bell.

Little Things, Big Differences

Let no debt remain outstanding, except the continuing debt to love one another, for he who loves his fellowman has fulfilled the law.

ROMANS 13:8

*M*y family and I spent a week in Disney World in Florida last summer. We traveled through Peter Pan's world, dove in a submarine, were chased by pirates, hugged Goofy. We visited Epcot Center and were transported through outer space. We witnessed 3-D movies and train wrecks at the MGM Studios. The children disappeared under six-foot waves at the man-made tidal wave pool in Typhoon Lagoon. We were carried by monorails, cable cars, steam trains, horse-drawn trolleys, but I think the best part of the Disney vacation was the parade.

Each night a spectacular parade of floats and people rolled down Main Street. All the people and all the floats were covered with strings of lights. But it wasn't the parade itself, or the lights, but something that happened one evening that I will always remember.

We were sitting on the curb, watching the parade. Karen, my ten-year-old daughter, was waving to all the characters that went by: Snow White, Chip and Dale, Mickey Mouse, but no one waved back. Then another collection of characters began to dance by. They were young women dressed in beautiful butterfly costumes. Well, Karen waved and waved, then, suddenly, one of the butterfly dancers nearly flew over and stood right before Karen. My daughter looked up and the butterfly stooped down and shook Karen's hand and asked, "Are you having fun?" in a beautiful southern accent. Karen said yes, and the butterfly flew away down Main Street.

That simple little thing was one of Karen's favorite moments in Disney World: one person making her feel special.

It is so easy to see what God expects from us if we just look closely at the actions of people around us. "Make every effort to add to your faith goodness; and to goodness, knowledge; and to knowledge, self-control; and to self-control, perseverance; and to perseverance, godliness; and to godliness, brotherly kindness; and to brotherly kindness, love. For if you possess these qualities in increasing measure, they will keep you from being ineffective and unproductive in your knowledge of our Lord Jesus Christ" (2 Pt 1:5-8).

The kindness the young woman demonstrated toward my daughter at the parade that night would surely earn a compliment from the managers of the Disney corporation.

It is easy to reach out to a stranger and make him or her feel special. During the day, ask the postman, or the doctor, or the person in line in front of you, if he or she is having a good day. It will make a bigger difference than you can imagine, and you will feel productive, effective, and you will earn a compliment from your day's manager: our Lord Jesus Christ.

Though I am humble, though I am small, though I am living my quiet life, I have power, Lord, to help others see. I have power Lord to help others smile. I have power Lord to be productive and effective in your work. I share the news! I share the news! You have risen Lord, and we are loved.

Singing and Ducking Muck Balls

You who dwell in the dust, wake up and shout for joy.

ISAIAH 26:19

$\mathcal{M}$y parents moved to this country from Belgium in 1948, so all my relatives live across the ocean. One summer, when I was a teenager, my grandmother sent me airfare so that I might visit the family I never knew.

I was able to spend a few weeks with my aunt and uncle in southern France. During the first night of my visit there was an extraordinary storm. The rain was heavy. Thunder and lightning fought all night between themselves, trying to see, it seemed, who had the most power.

The next morning I met my uncle at the breakfast table. "Your aunt is in the attic cleaning up the mess. She won't let me help. See what you can do."

I walked up the attic stairs and there I found my aunt scooping up dirt and muck from the floor. The roof leaked the night before. Water spilled into the old attic. My aunt was sopping up the filth and dropping it into a bucket. She was filthy. She looked horrible, and she was laughing and singing. I thought she was crazy.

"But, Christopher," she said. "I spent many years in a prison camp during the war. It was horrible. No work for me today is unpleasant. Come join me."

I spent the whole morning singing with my aunt. We threw muck balls at each other. We laughed. By lunchtime the attic was clean.

Did you ever have an experience that hurt you? We are not born to suffer. Difficult things happen to us all, but those things are not who we are. Faith in God lifts us beyond our sorrows. Each day we can say aloud to the Lord: "My comfort in my suffering is this: Your promise preserves my life" (Ps 119:50).

We are meant to laugh and to sing. Try it. Join my aunt in the attic today and praise God.

Dear God pour your water on my suffering so my suffering turns to wine. Let me drink to you my Lord. I make a toast to the promise. I bow down in your presence. My pain is my garment. May we dance and shout in joy?

The Stability of God in Our Lives

"Surely I have acted like a fool."

1 SAMUEL 26:21

One of the gifts I bought for my daughter's birthday was a volleyball set. I noticed a few days before her birthday that the children were playing their own version of the game using a beach ball and the backyard fence as their net.

I drove to the sporting goods store and asked a salesman if he could help me pick out a good set.

We walked down an aisle filled with baseball bats, hockey sticks, lawn games, sneakers, until he pointed to a shelf with four types of volleyball equipment stored in boxes.

"Which one is the best?" I asked.

"Well, the ones with the thickest poles are good. Perhaps you'd like this set that also includes rackets for badminton. It's our most popular seller."

I bought the most popular seller, brought it home, wrapped it up, and placed it on the dining room table along with the other presents for Karen's party.

The next day, after the cake, the songs, and the opening of presents, I sat on the back lawn with the open box, trying to understand the instructions for erecting the volleyball net.

A frustrating hour later, the net was up and the ball was inflated. The children played the rest of the afternoon, bouncing the ball over the net, then switching to the badminton rackets. It had been a good birthday.

I slept late the next morning and was awakened with the sound of laughter. I opened my shade and looked down in the yard, and there were the children, bouncing the beach ball back and forth over the backyard fence.

We have to be careful about what we want to improve in the world. Christ came to us to redirect our vision toward God in heaven and away from man-made gods: money, envy, power, faithlessness. Some things ought not change: good memories, love, faith in the risen Lord.

If you are planning to make something better today, take a close look at what it is you want to do and ask yourself, "Is it really necessary?" Maybe we can take delight in celebrating the way things are instead of trying to make them into something that they ought not be.

As the air, as the soil, as the water abounds throughout the earth, so too your presence Lord surrounds my life without fail. Is it possible Lord, is it wonderfully possible that I could be so blessed in the continuity of your divine love? I know the answer is yes, and yes I say to you for in my answer to your call I know I am secure.

Loving Your Neighbor

But a Samaritan, as he traveled, came where the man was; and when he saw him, he took pity on him. He went to him and band-aged his wounds.

LUKE 10:33-34

I was home alone with the children: five-year-old David, three-year-old Karen, and Michael, the infant. Roe was at work, her two-nights-a-week position as a receptionist for an orthodontist. Just before dinner I realized that Karen had developed a high fever.

Perhaps I should take her to the doctor, I thought. Roe agreed for I had called her at work for an opinion. After I hung up the phone, I walked out of the kitchen and found Karen slumped on the living room couch. She was facing the ceiling and foaming at the mouth. Her eyes were rolled back. She was still and unconscious. I thought she was dying.

I didn't know what to do. Michael wasn't walking yet. David was bewildered. I simply wanted to run into the street and scream for help. I did scream: "Karen! Karen! Karen!" She wasn't responding.

The telephone. I called the police, the ambulance.

I rushed about through the dining room, through the living room, holding Karen, calling her name again and again, but there was still no response.

A minute later, I called the police again. "Please hurry," but, before I could place the receiver back in its place, the doorbell rang.

Red and blue lights flashed throughout the neighborhood. I quickly answered the solid knocking and there, standing before me, stood the tallest, broadest giant of a policeman I had ever seen. I could smell his leather coat. His shoes were shined. I wanted to hug him.

"I don't know what happened to my daughter! She isn't responding!"

"She's having a seizure," the policeman said in a low, confident voice. "Is she ill?"

"She has a fever! I know that! I was about to call the doctor!"

The policeman peacefully entered the house. "Let's take her upstairs and run some cool water in the bathtub. We need to bring her fever down a bit."

I pointed to the stairs. The policeman walked up, entered the bathroom, and began running the water. I was not aware that three or four neighbors had entered the house and were tending to David and Michael. I was not aware that the ambulance was on its way. All I knew was that a stranger was lifting my daughter out of my arms and gently placing her in a tepid tub of water.

I knelt on the floor to the left of the policeman. He, too, was kneeling and leaning over the wall of the bathtub scooping up handfuls of water and slowly pouring them over Karen's hot back. His gun was belted to his waist. His badge scraped against the porcelain. As he was tending to Karen, he turned to me and whispered, "I have a three-year-old daughter, too."

Karen began to respond. I dried her with a towel, dropped it on the floor and wrapped her in a wool blanket, and then I carried her downstairs. My neighbors said they would watch over the boys. The ambulance drove onto the front lawn and right up to the front door. Two-way radios squawked in the background.

After I again wrapped Karen in the blanket, after I stepped into the ambulance through that wide, rear door, after I sat down and held Karen against my chest, I cried and I cried.

The emergency room doctor said that Karen had suffered a febrile seizure, which some young children are prone to. A consultation with our family doctor was suggested. Her temperature dropped. Karen was fine.

In Tennessee Williams' play "The Glass Menagerie," Amanda the mother tells her son, "We have to do all that we can to build ourselves up. In these trying times we live in, all that we have to cling to is each other."

After my daughter was safely tucked in bed that night, as I walked past the bathroom, I noticed that our policeman had drained the bathtub and folded the towels.

This policeman, my policeman had no reason to be so kind, so interested, so caring, but like the Good Samaritan, he stopped his regular routine and felt compassion for me and for my daughter.

Jesus told the story about the Samaritan because he wanted to give an example of the type of people who will be rewarded eternal peace in heaven: those who love their neighbors for no reward.

Why don't you send in a friendship card a hundred dollars today to someone you know who needs the money, but do not sign the card? It will be money in your pocket. Or volunteer your services at the local hospital once a week. It will be your best health care insurance. Give of yourself in the name of compassion, in the name of the Lord, and you will be rewarded.

Silence in my actions, silence in my love creates a symphony for the Lord.

When Plans Succeed

Plans fail for lack of counsel, but with many advisers they succeed.
PROVERBS 15:22

I wanted to take the children to the circus. Better yet, I planned to take them to the greatest circus in the world in one of the greatest cities of the world, New York.

I bought the tickets, not realizing they were for the same day Roe planned to take the children to the eye doctor, so she had to rearrange the schedule.

I waved the tickets above my head when I came home that night after I made my purchase for ringside seats.

"The circus! We're going to the circus!" I announced.

"I don't want to go," my daughter quietly said.

"Why not?" I asked.

"Remember the last time? I'm afraid of the man on stilts."

"I'm not going," my older son said, "if I have to hear her complain the whole time."

Michael, the youngest, looked up and asked, "What's a circus?"

Three weeks later I was in the car driving to New York with two children who had low fevers, one child who decided she wasn't going to open her eyes the whole time, and Roe who teased me saying, "Maybe we would have had a better time at the eye doctor's."

Have you ever stepped into a difficult situation because you didn't make plans? Do you ever want to do something simply because you want to do it without asking anyone what they think?

163

We need advice. We need to explain our ideas to others before they are explained to the world. Christ selected his apostles to listen to his ideas about how the world ought to be. Well, those twelve listened, asked the Lord questions, and then they slowly understood what Christ was saying. I think Christ's plan succeeded for he sought counsel, not openly from his apostles, but from God.

If you are planning to do something today, ask yourself, "Did I ask those involved for ideas? Did I include others in my plan?"

And what about your eternal plans? Did you share your ideas with God today? Did you seek his counsel?

I need to plan the evening meal, plan my visit to the post office. I need to plan for the children's lunch, and their ride home from school. I need to plan my presentation at work. I need to plan for the next purchase order. My Lord God as I prepare myself for the day let me say that I also prepare myself for you, for I choose to succeed in your eyes.

Is Anyone Home?

The Lord God said, "It is not good for the man to be alone."

GENESIS 2:18

*A*fter a long day at work, I was pleased to step out of the building. The car was cold. I brushed the freshly fallen snow from the windshield. It was dark, and I was tired.

As I drove along the streets, I looked out my window and thought about other people driving home at night in this same cold. Could other people feel as tired as I did? Could other people be looking at me through their car windows wondering what I felt like?

I drove down the main street of my town, turned left, continued on my way through a yellow blinking light, made another left-hand turn, and pulled into my driveway.

I reached my briefcase from the backseat and dragged myself up the side stairs. The door was locked. I fished in my pocket, retrieved my set of keys, inserted the gray key into the lock, turned the key, and then I stepped into the house.

"Hi everyone. I'm home!" The wind whipped the screen door against the railing outside. I reached out and closed the two doors.

"Hello!" I called out once again. Mittens the cat ran in from the living room and rubbed against my legs. I brushed her aside. She was shedding orange fur all over my new suit.

"Is anyone home?" I called out, just as I walked into the kitchen and found a note from Roe explaining that she and the children drove to the mall and would be shopping and having dinner.

I opened the refrigerator door and rummaged around for dinner: a cold chicken leg, noodles, and a salad.

The house was silent. The rooms were empty. Again Mittens rubbed against me, and I was about to push her away again to protect my suit, but then she began to purr, so I leaned over and picked her up in my arms and began petting her under the chin. I broke off a piece of chicken and gave it to her. If she could, Mittens would have said thank you. She rubbed against my jacket, jumped off my lap, and ate the chicken with obvious delight.

After my lonely evening, Roe and the children finally returned. The back door burst open like a popped balloon. "Daddy! We're home," Michael yelled.

"Look at my new dress," Karen said waving a bag above her head. David, my oldest son, rolled his eyes.

When Roe entered the house she kissed me then said, "Chris, your suit is a mess. It's covered with Mittens' hair."

"I know," I said. "It's nice in a way. Shows she's around. I missed you."

"Come see Karen's dress," she answered, leading me by the hand toward the loud and full living room. Mittens cried to be let out. Her job was done.

Can you imagine how lonely Adam was without anyone there to keep him company? We are all alone in certain ways. Some of us live by ourselves, and others can be in a place full of people and still feel alone. But if we call out and say "I am lonely" someone will listen, especially God.

Tell a friend today, tell your husband or wife, tell your children that you are in need of their company, and they will come to you as the Lord comes to you each time you ask.

I am lonely, I am lonely, I am sometimes lonely Lord, but I am never alone for you are always in my heart and in my home. I am not afraid because I seek your companionship each day.

Protect What Is Small in God's Vast Kingdom

But ask the animals, and they will teach you, or the birds of the air, and they will tell you; or speak to the earth, and it will teach you, or let the fish of the sea inform you. Which of all these does not know that the hand of the Lord has done this?

JOB 12:7-9

I was ten years old and too young to understand the meaning of goals or perseverance. One night, just after I turned off my light, as my head pressed against my pillow, I thought I heard a noise, a distant sound, an animal sound, perhaps a scratching, then a small cry. Then I slept.

The next morning, while pulling on my socks, I heard again a slight scratching and a slight cry. Surely, there was something. I looked under my bed. Dust and comic books. I looked out my window. Maple tree. Wisteria vine.

Again, a slight scratching.

My room at the time was on the third floor beside the attic. I walked up to the attic door and listened. Yes, a scratching. I pressed my ear against the door. Yes, a small cry. The light switch was under my fingertip. I opened the door. Trunks, old coats, a bookcase. Silence.

Just as I was about to return to my room, I heard, with more clarity, the same scratching sound and cry, a screeching sound perhaps.

The ceiling of the attic took the shape of the roof: high peaked, slanting down toward the floor. I walked to my right, stepping over National Geographic magazines, past an old bathtub. The floor ended just at the edge where the roof ended. I found a large hole in the roof and a large pile of grass and twigs. An abandoned nest. Beyond the nest was the dark hole, the top of the wall space which ran down to the first floor.

Scratching. Crying. An empty nest. Perhaps? I ran back to my room, picked out a flashlight and a hand mirror from my box of treasures and ran back to the hole. Because the roof was angled down so close to the floor, I had to rest flat on my back, hold the mirror above my head, and aim the flashlight beam down the wall. There, in the reflection in the mirror, down the three-story space between the wall, I saw a bird, a young bird—a starling.

How many days had it been inside the wall? I quickly stood up and looked around the attic. I found a small, straw basket. I broke the sides of the basket which created what I was looking for: a small, flat platform with a handle. I then tied a rope to the handle. I wiggled onto my back once again, adjusted the mirror, wedged the flashlight into the space so I didn't have to hold it. Then I slowly lowered my platform on a rope. Slowly, slowly, the small, broken basket wiggled closer and closer to the bird.

The room was hot. My back hurt. I realized I was under a spider-web. No one knew a little boy was in the attic trying to rescue a starling. I managed to lower the basket just within inches of the bird. Then I continued to drop it even lower until the platform rested right on the creature. What happened is what I had hoped would happen. Because there wasn't any space for the bird to escape, it started to shake, move, adjust its position as the basket pressed upon the bird until the platform was flat upon the bottom of the shaft, and the bird simply wiggled on to the platform for lack of any other place to sit.

Slowly, slowly, I began to pull the bird up and up. Slowly, slowly, until I reached down into the hole and held the bird in my hand. No magician could feel the same wonder I felt as I pulled the bird out of the darkness and held it up to the light. It squawked and kicked and squawked some more. It was too young to fly, but old enough to be fed bits of meat and water, which it accepted eagerly.

My parents were proud of me when I told them what I had done. My sisters and brothers didn't believe me and thought I just took the bird from the nest.

Two months later, I opened my bedroom window. The starling, plump, full of feathers and energy, sat on my extended finger. I pushed my hand out the window. The bird held fast. I shook my hand a bit. The bird wobbled, flapped its wings vigorously, fell forward, extended those wings, quickly looped upward and flew into the maple tree.

I leaned my arms against the windowsill. Then I placed my chin on my arms and looked at my starling. It twisted its head back and forth, and wiped its beak against the tree branch.

I liked what I did.

If, as the Bible says, "in [God's] hand is the life of every creature and the breath of all mankind" (Job 12:10), it seems to make sense for a person to tend to an injured bird.

This might seem like an odd suggestion, but see if you can find a small creature that needs your assistance today: a trapped fly in the office, a worm washed up on the sidewalk, a ladybug stuck inside your kitchen window. Catch the fly and release. Carry the worm back to the soil. Open the kitchen window and flick the ladybug back into the yard. If we pay attention to these small creatures, we will know the Creator a bit better. They might speak to us, tell us, teach us that, indeed, the Lord has done this.

Bless the fish and sea creatures; bless the sparrows. Bless my life and soul, Lord of the sheep and the lions, God of the great tigers and the small insects. God bless all living things.

Slow to Speak, Slow to Anger

A hot-tempered man stirs up dissension, but a patient man calms a quarrel.

PROVERBS 15:18

One hot morning I was sitting on the deck reading the newspaper when I heard this loud, irritating whirring noise. I turned the page of the paper, expecting the noise to stop after awhile.

By the time I finished the last page of the newspaper, the irritating noise still cluttered the peaceful neighborhood.

I stood up from my chair and stepped around the corner of the house. The noise increased its volume. I looked to my left. Nothing. I looked to my right. Nothing. I looked up, and there it was, a fan, an attic fan in my neighbor's house whirring, clanking, making a terrible, citylike racket.

My neighbor had installed the fan the day before. I was angry. How can anyone disturb the peace with such a machine, I asked myself. And couldn't he have installed it on the opposite side of his house?

For days I stomped around the house, complaining to my wife about this noise, this fan, this inconvenient, irritating nuisance.

Finally, after a week, I was fed up. I walked over to my neighbor's house, and rang the doorbell. My defense was prepared. My anger was controlled. I was going to ask him to disconnect that fan.

"Hi, Chris," my neighbor warmly greeted me. "Come on in."

"How are you, Jerry?" I said as we shook hands.

"Well, better," he said. "We've had a bit of a scare the last few weeks. Anna (Jerry's daughter) developed a terrible breathing problem. The doctor suggested fresh air, not air-conditioning, at night so I installed an attic fan. Anna now, finally sleeps at night again so all is okay again."

Jerry looked at me. I looked at him, then he asked, "What's new with you?"

"Well," I said, "I, ah, was wondering if I could borrow your hedge clippers."

When I returned to my house, I clipped the bushes, swept the driveway, drove to town, bought the newspaper and sat on my deck for the rest of the afternoon.

The noisy fan has never bothered me since.

"My dear brothers, take note of this: Everyone should be quick to listen, slow to speak and slow to become angry, for man's anger does not bring about the righteous life that God desires" (Jas 1:19-20).

If you are angry with someone try and figure out today what is the cause of your anger. And try to discover why that person does what he or she does that angers you so.

If you take the energy you use to be angry and use it to work toward peace, there will be peace.

May the Lord be with me in my relationships with those that I know and meet. May the Lord help me see what he sees in us all: goodness, beauty, innocence. May the Lord grant me tolerance. For these things I pray.

Thanks in Everything

I will give you a wise and discerning heart.

1 KINGS 3:12

One morning in autumn my mother called me to her sewing room. I was a little boy full of energy and rough ways: I liked to chase my sisters with mud balls at that time.

"Christopher, I just finished knitting you this sweater. Let's try it on."

I remember I wore a checkered shirt. The sweater was red and gray, a sleeveless vest with buttons in the front.

As my mother slipped the sweater on, I looked over her shoulder and made a funny face in the mirror behind her. My sisters called me "Dopey" when I was a child because of my huge ears. My ears stuck out, especially with the type of haircut from the late 1950s. My baby-sitter said that my ears were so big because my older brother pulled on them so often.

I was the type of child who didn't take big ears so seriously. (I secretly imagined if I could flap them hard enough, I could fly like Dumbo.)

"Now," my mother said as she adjusted the sweater. "Look at yourself."

I stood before her mirror and looked like Dopey with a baggy sweater. It looked awful, but my mother made it so I loved it.

Later in the afternoon, when I was in the yard jumping into the pile of leaves my father collected, I noticed something. My buttons from the sweater had faces. Each button had two eyes, a nose, and a smile.

I ran into the kitchen and showed my mother the wonderful buttons. She embraced me. I wondered why.

Of course I now understand why a mother would embrace a child who took free delight in something she did. I know with certitude my mother taught me to be grateful for what I have.

Are you grateful for all your blessings? Today rise up, "sing and make music in your heart to the Lord, always giving thanks to God the Father for everything" (Eph 5:19-20).

Perhaps as a gesture of gratitude, you can make a gift for someone you love, and add a secret extra something, like buttons with smiles.

I am grateful Lord. I am grateful, Father. I am grateful my God for all that I am, for all that I do and see, for all that is possible. I am grateful to you for everything. Thank you and thank you. I bow my head and say thank you.

It Was Very Good

A man will leave his father and mother and be united to his wife, and they will become one flesh.

GENESIS 2:24

*A*s I walked to town for the Saturday newspaper I found a wedding ring on the side of the road. Roe and the children were still sleeping. I was awake and anxious. The new spring season had just exploded. The earth smelled rich and moist. The flowers were in bloom.

There is a stillness in a spring morning. The sky retains a soft blue. The sun is at the beginning of its full strength.

I like the silence at such times. I like the sense of loneliness. No man or woman lives without loneliness. Even among those we love we discover there is still a place in the heart that is not satisfied. Perhaps this feeling of emptiness is what makes someone write a book or sing a song. We make attempts each day to fill in the empty places in our hearts.

Halfway to the newspaper store, I saw a bit of color in the dirt. I leaned over and picked up a gold ring, a wedding ring.

I can imagine what it is like for an archeologist to discover a bowl or an earring or an ancient tool deep inside a ceremonial cave. I can imagine the scientist trying to figure out what these artifacts means, who owned them, what was their purpose.

The ring I found belonged to a woman. It was thin and small. Engraved on the inside were two names: Harry and Eve.

Did Eve toss the ring out of Harry's car? Did Harry anger Eve? Did Eve accept defeat in the relationship? Did Harry toss the ring out the window? Did Eve anger Harry? Did Harry accept defeat in the relationship?

I rolled the ring in my palm a few times, then I stuck it in my pocket and continued on my way.

By the time I arrived at the newspaper store, I had forgotten about the ring. I picked up the newspaper from the stacks, paid my money, and walked out of the store.

As I quickly scanned the headlines, I heard a crazy cry from the distant lake. There, in the middle of the water I saw two small black dots. I walked a bit closer to the lake when the foolish cry began again; then one of the black dots turned into a pair of wings flapping over the water's surface.

Loons! Two loons!

I folded the newspaper under my arm and walked to the edge of the lake and sat on a bench. I watched the two birds swim together. At times they disappeared under the water and reappeared moments later. Again one of the birds gave out its loud cry. Was it a cry of love? A cry of anger? A cry in welcome to the new spring? I cupped my hands around my mouth and called out, "Hello Harry! Hello Eve!" The loons paid no attention.

By the time I returned from my walk, Roe was downstairs in the kitchen. The children were still sleeping.

"What's new?" she asked, as she often does when I return home with the newspaper. I walked up to her side, gave her a kiss, then I said, "Nothing much. Just a pair of loons waking up together down on the lake."

How sad to think that two people lost a ring. That perhaps two people lost their love for each other.

Love binds. It is what God wants for us. We leave our childhood and our parents so that we can strike out into a new journey, with a wife or husband. We live with loneliness, but "God created man in his own image, in the image of God he created him; male and female he created them" (Gn 1:27). We find solace in the embrace of those we love. God made us. He understood our need for love. He created us for love. "God saw all that he had made, and it was very good" (Gn 1:31).

I sent the ring to the police station, thinking that perhaps someone might return to look for it. No one did.

A policeman drove to the house one afternoon and returned the ring. "Sad, isn't it?" he asked. "Someone losing their wedding ring?"

Yes, I agreed as I heard the children in the house playing with the dog, and Roe talking in the background on the phone with her friend Linda.

In the end we always return to those we love. Embrace your husband or wife this evening. Call up a mother or father and wish them a good night. And, in the end, there is always God. You are never alone. And that is very good.

In the union of marriage, there is God. In the union of life and death, there is God. In the union of parents and their children, there is God. In the union between friends, there is God. Thank you Lord Jesus for your word "I will give you the keys of the kingdom of heaven; whatever you bind on earth will be bound in heaven" (Mt 16:19). Thank you God for the keys to your heart. In this I pray.

Do Not Rage Against the Dying of the Light

The people living in darkness have seen a great light; on those liv-
ing in the land of the shadow of death a light has dawned.

MATTHEW 4:16

*D*uring the final illness of D.J. Thomas, his son, Dylan, wrote the famous poem, "Do Not Go Gentle into That Good Night." It is this poem that I thought about two days after Fred Rogers died of stomach cancer.

For the past eighteen years, Fred sent me letters every week, called me on the phone every last Saturday of the month, and e-mailed me every day when e-mail entered into our lives.

When I turned fifty, Fred gave me the gold cuff links his father gave him when he turned fifty. This Christmas Fred sent me candlesticks that he bought at Nantucket. I sent him my poems, copies of my new books, pictures of my children, letters about my loneliness and dreams. Fred and I spoke about our wives and chil-dren. He'd tell me about seeing the moon during his evening walks, or about a book he was reading. I would tell him about the tree that fell on our neighbor's house, or about my daughter's high school band concert. He would tell me that his son "J" and the grand-children were coming for pizza.

When I met Fred eighteen years ago in New York, he and I were placed, alone, in the "Greenroom" at the HBO studios for an hour. I was working on a pilot children's television program that never aired, and Fred was coming to the studio for an interview.

We never met before. We shook hands, and then we began to talk about who we were. He told me about his wife Joanne and how much he loves her, and Fred told me about his sons and how much he loves them. Then he took out his wallet and showed me their pictures. I told him about my wife Roe and about our two children. We laughed a bit. I liked the man. When we said good-bye, Fred suggested that I come to Pittsburgh someday and visit.

That visit turned out to be an invitation a few weeks later to do a taping with Fred and with May Sarton on Fred's television neighborhood.

We became fast friends, Fred and I, and a few years later, I asked him why.

"Chris, when I first met you, you seemed to like me for me. You didn't want me to endorse anything. You didn't want anything from me. You were interested in my children and in my wife, and you cared about me." I liked the man.

I remember being with Fred at his summer home at Nantucket. He introduced me to his lovely sister, and he brought me to one of his favorite spots, the tip of the island where the dunes were high. We sat on a log and he told me about his father, and how much he loved his father, and how much his father liked this place, this very spot. I told Fred about my father, how much he loved us all, and how old he now was, and how much I miss sailing with my father on the wide rivers of Ontario. Then Fred and I went swimming.

After our swim, we sat in the summer chairs on the deck to his little house. Fred worked on the upcoming scripts for his television neighborhood, I was working on the manuscript of one of my new books. Suddenly, a seagull flew down from the sky and perched itself on a pillar three feet from where I sat. "Hello," said the seagull, in a very familiar seagull voice. I looked up from my manuscript and smiled. "Hello," I said.

"What ya doing?" asked the seagull.

"I'm working on a new collection of essays."

"You don't look like you're working very hard," the seagull laughed, and then the laugh turned into the laugh of Fred, and I turned to the man who created the voices of those famous little puppets, and we laughed some more and we felt just fine.

I lost my best friend last Thursday morning, and when I went to the high school where I work, I heard so many students talking about Mr. Rogers dying. A teacher openly wept in the hall when she heard the news. And then I suddenly remembered that I was not the only one who lost a friend.

George Washington is considered the father of our country, and for the past thirty-five years, Fred Rogers has been the father of our souls, reminding us that we are likable just the way we are, reminding us that it is such a good feeling to know that we are alive, and reminding us that we are special on the outside, and we are special on the inside.

Dylan Thomas was angry that his father died, and demanded that we rage and rage against the dying of the light. Fred reminded me for the past eighteen years to celebrate the birth of light each day.

Dylan Thomas said that "wise men at their end know dark is right." Fred Rogers reminded us all that light is what is important, and goodness, gentleness, compassion, self-confidence, courage, and love.

At the end of many phone conversations, Fred would often say to me with his sure faith, "Chris, you know who is in charge." This is what Fred Rogers said to us all each day of his life. And we can now say to him in return, "Do, by all means, do go gently into that good night."

Holy God, we praise your name as we live; we whisper your name in the room of our death, and you call out our names as we enter your neighborhood. For this we give thanks, for this we pray to your name of names.

Midsummer Night's Dream

At that time Jesus said, "I praise you, Father, Lord of heaven and earth, because you have hidden these things from the wise and learned, and revealed them to little children.

MATTHEW 11:25

I do not know exactly when it happened, but I know that the boy in me is completely gone.

I remember sitting in Mrs. MacGinnis' cherry tree with my sister Anne as we picked cherries and laughed and laughed as we spit out the pits onto the grass below our dangling feet.

One summer my brother and I built a tree fort in the woods. We lined the floor with bits of old carpet, made a screened window, and nailed real shingles on the roof. The night we slept in the fort, we looked for glowing wood under rotting logs, caught bullfrogs, and roasted potatoes in the campfire we made in the clearing just to the left of the tree house.

When it was hot outside, we set up the Slip 'n Slide, my sisters and brothers and I, and we rolled our smooth bodies along the wet plastic sheet that spread out along the grass, and we giggled, splashed each other and we felt just fine.

Even the moon was on our side when we were children, guiding us along the way during our night games of hide-and-seek or reflecting against our faces as my sister and I sat out on the roof outside her window and watched the bats zigzagging in the blue-black sky above our heads.

When my own children were young, we retrieved the Ragu bottle from the garbage can, rinsed it out, poked holes in the lid and chased after fireflies. I remember how the children ran to the house, turned off all the lights and showed their mother how the fireflies glowed in the Ragu jar. "Hey, we could read a book if we put it real close to the jar," my daughter said, and she pulled down a book from the shelf, opened the pages and we all tried to read the words. And when we released the fireflies before going to bed, the children and I sang a song, shooing the flashing insects on their way.

I once wore Davy Crocket hats, baseball caps, Keds sneakers. I chewed Bazooka bubble gum, read Superman comic books, shot firecrackers on July 4th, bought a chocolate eclair from the Good Humor truck once a week, made daisy crowns, ate saltwater taffy, sold Kool-Aid on the sidewalk, rode my bike to town with Johnny, my best friend, and we bought Ring Dings or Devil Dogs all during the summer.

The rope swing over the lake, Devil's Cave to explore, ferns, robins' eggs, apple fights, salamander hunts, kites that never flew, girls who never kissed, marbles in the dust, Turkish Taffy, raccoons in the garbage cans, marathon Monopoly games, thunderstorms, summer, hot, open, summer, a place for boys to be pirates, and for girls to be not quite pirates, but nearly so.

My three children have grown up. One is engaged. Two are in college. I haven't slept in a tree fort in forty years or chased after a firefly in fifteen years. I check the thermometer outside my window and see it is ninety-eight degrees.

I lie at night in my bed as the fan whirrs, and the hot air flows around the room like an invisible dragon. I look out my open window and see the summer moon and close my eyes, and then I dream that there is a boy out there in his Keds sneakers selling Kool-Aid. I think that I am ready to be a grandfather.

Thank you Lord for allowing me to remember the ways of the child, for letting me keep my eyes and smile of a child, for it is in the child where the soul resides; for this I am glad.

A Child Is Born

Let's go to Bethlehem.

LUKE 2:15

*E*ach December in the days when I was young, the congregation of the Presbyterian church down the road built a manger, spread real straw on the floor, and arranged in the new construction life-size figures of the Holy Family, two sheep, a donkey, shepherds, and three kings. It was part of our family's tradition in the Christmas season to visit this crèche.

Early one December when I was nine years old, my father announced that we were going to walk downtown and pay our respects to the baby Jesus. This visit was unique because we walked to the church after dark. In the past we always drove to the manger scene because it was too cold to walk, and there was always a baby in our family that prevented us from pursuing much adventure. When I was nine, the baby was four, could walk on her own, and wanted to carry the flashlight.

"Everyone take a hat and gloves. It's very cold," my mother announced as she reached into the closet for our coats.

We walked out of the house and proceeded to follow my four-year-old sister in single file down the sidewalk. Now that I look back it was like following a star, in a way, the star of Bethlehem in the hands of my little sister leading us to the newborn King.

By the time we arrived at the manger, my father was carrying my sister in his arms and the flashlight batteries died, but the church

186

erected soft lights that illuminated the ancient scene that stood before us. My mother reminded us that we celebrate Christmas as a reminder of Christ's birthday. She retold the story of Mary and Joseph, how they were searching for a vacant inn. While my mother spoke about the manger, I leaned over and touched the robe of one of the three kings. To my surprise, a small yellow piece of the robe broke off and fell into my hand. I didn't know what to do with it. I didn't want to tell my parents because I was afraid that they might be angry that I ripped the robe of one of the three kings. I didn't want to drop the piece of cloth because I felt it was sacrilegious, like dropping the American flag to the ground, so I quickly stuck the yellow bit of cloth into my pocket just as my mother finished telling us about the angels and the arrival of the three kings.

"Time to go home," my father announced as he rearranged my sleeping sister on his shoulder.

That night my sisters and brothers, my mother and father and I walked home in the dark. As we entered the house, my father flicked on a single lamp in the living room so that we could find our way upstairs and to our beds.

After brushing our teeth, after slipping into our pajamas, and after kissing my parents good night, I pulled the yellow piece of cloth out of my pants pocket and slipped it under my pillow.

The three wise men also followed a light many years ago. What they found at the end of their journey was a child who filled them with immense joy. They kneeled down before the child. Perhaps they smiled, nodded their heads in approval, praised Mary and Joseph. These three kings stepped back and unwrapped the gifts they brought: gold, frankincense, and myrrh. This is what my mother told me.

I kept the yellow piece of cloth from the robe of the wise man for many years. Perhaps it was a gift. I believed for a time that the cloth had magical powers, perhaps the power to keep my hands warm, or the power to illuminate a dark room.

Today I understand the true gift of the Magi: the Christmas faith, the image of Mary and Joseph protecting the baby, my father carrying my sister home on his back.

We all have bits of the wise man's cloth in our hands. It is our responsibility to use this gift, to believe in its power, to be humble in the reality that something significant happened a little over two thousand years ago in the small town of Bethlehem. It is our faith. It is our salvation.

"I bring you good news of great joy that will be for all the people," the angels said to the shepherds. "Today in the town of David a Savior has been born to you; he is Christ the Lord" (Lk 2:10-11).

Today, and every day, enjoy the simple wonder of the Lord. Glory to God in the highest, and peace on earth and goodwill to all. Today let us go to Bethlehem.

Glory to God, and glory to God. In thanks for the Good News for all time and for all people, let us raise our hands in glory, great glory to God.

A Marzipan Strawberry and a Tin Alligator

Know how to give good gifts to your children.

LUKE 11:13

A few nights ago, in the quiet darkness of my fiftieth December, my wife and I returned home from Christmas shopping. As I turned off the engine of the car, I said, "I think I see Norman Rockwell peeking out the upstairs window."

She and I had spent the morning hanging Christmas wreaths outside each window of our four-bedroom colonial. A red ribbon hangs from each wreath. We have a single, electric candle in each window, and a spotlight illuminating the entire façade of the house. An American flag hangs motionless to the right of the front door.

It is easy to see why our little house could be on the front cover of the old *Saturday Evening Post.* We, in this country, try hard to re-create Christmas the way it used to be, or the way we imagine it was.

For Christmas one year I received six lead soldiers, British loyalists cast in rigid marching positions, each holding a bayoneted rifle, and each wearing a red coat and a tall hat that looked like a black olive.

Every Christmas when I was a boy my stocking contained marzipan fruit, chocolate coins wrapped in gold, a bird call or a plastic submarine that rose and sank in the bathtub with baking soda fuel.

My mother sewed my stocking the year I was born. It was a giant sock, made of white cloth with prints of clowns and sprawling circus dogs. She attached six little jingle bells to the stocking: red, green, blue, and silver bells. I especially liked the one that was sewn at the tip of the toe.

For many years as a boy all I wanted for Christmas was a set of walkie-talkies, which I never received.

When I was ten my mother gave me Sterling North's book, *Rascal*. My father gave me a toy safe made of gray metal with a red combination dial. My grandmother gave me a Lincoln Logs set, and my aunt sent over from Belgium a glass snow globe that, when you shook it, revealed a small snowman with a black top hat standing in the swirl of little flakes that floated around his stout belly.

I liked magic tricks for Christmas, especially the one where the ball in the small plastic urn appeared and disappeared with a slight twist of the fingers. I liked the windup tin alligator from my brother, and the glow-in-the-dark superball from my sister.

This afternoon my wife and I drove our three grown children to Pennsylvania to cut down our twenty-fifth Christmas tree. We, as usual, disagreed on the height, the width, the shape. After much deliberation we agreed on the one my eighteen-year-old daughter marked with her scarf in the first place. I cut down the tree, and the two boys helped me carry it to the car. We sang Christmas songs, and as we drove through town, I saw that Robbie Jones once again posed the plywood Santa Claus and the eight reindeer along the rooftop of his hardware store.

As we pulled into the driveway, my wife said she would make hot chocolate. I turned off the engine as everyone stepped out of the car and started walking down the driveway. I sat for a moment, leaned against the steering wheel, looked out the windshield and thought

I saw, peeking through the upstairs window, a little boy with a walkie-talkie pressed against his left ear, and then my twenty-two-year-old son turned around and called, "Come on, Dad."

I hope I find in my stocking this year a large marzipan strawberry and a tin alligator.

For the gift of your birth, we thank you, Lord. For the gift of your message, we praise you.

Spring Is Just Around the Corner

If you remain in me and my words remain in you, ask whatever you wish, and it will be given you.

JOHN 15:7

I am haunted by a spring season that I cannot define. I remember seeing my grandmother sitting on a lawn chair in the backyard with the newspaper spread out on her lap. I am walking down the driveway, with my chemistry book and *The Great Gatsby* under my arm. I can hear the distant Eric Lackawanna train passing through town. I must have been seventeen. It was two months before Woodstock. In a few weeks a man would walk on the moon for the first time. I had a date with Aileen that night, so it must have been a Friday.

It has been cold these past many weeks. This morning I found a dead, frozen squirrel laying on its back in the middle of the lawn. My guess is it fell from its nest and hit the frozen ground and died instantly. The New York harbor is choked with ice. There has been snow on the ground since Christmas. We pull into ourselves when we are cold, and conjure up a certain nostalgia for summer heat and lemonade.

Two weeks ago my sister-in-law gave a surprise birthday party for her husband who just turned fifty. My wife Roe and I joined in on the surprise and drove to Helene's house in south Jersey. As I pulled into the driveway and shut off the engine, I heard a distinct honking of geese somewhere in the distance. I stepped out of the car and looked across the road to a small lake. It was already dark, so I strained my eyes and saw, in the middle of the lake, a wide stretch of ice and snow, and the vague outline of a few geese.

As Roe and I entered the house, I said to Helene, "I didn't realize it was so cold. That is a *huge* sheet of ice on the lake. And all that snow layered on top."

Helene looked at me and said, "What ice?"

"On your lake. All that snow in the middle of the lake piled on the ice."

"Chris," Helene said. "That's not snow and ice. That is hundreds of snow geese."

"Snow geese! Here? But how is that possible?" I went outside again, hopped into the car, turned it around to face the center of the lake, and then I turned on the headlights. The geese started honking and flapping their wings and this huge pile of ice and snow turned into an annoyed stadium of excited snow geese. I had never seen a snow goose.

"Look, Roe!" I said as she came outside to join me. "Look how beautiful!"

"Helene said that they will be here for just a few days. They're migrating. They start out in the Arctic regions of North America and eastern Siberia."

So I too migrate from season to season, from one end of my life to the other traveling 408 months back to my senior prom. Where is the spring of comfort?

Last night I walked the dog around the neighborhood. We usually let her run freely in the fenced yard, but last night, the dog was a bit restless.

As we passed a few houses, I distinctly heard a sound I had not heard in many years: ice skates clicking against the ice. I was sure that is what it was, even though there was not a pond or lake in the neighborhood. But how was it possible that I heard ice skates, and then I heard children laughing.

When I reached the next house, there they were: three children skating on the small ice-skating rink their father installed in their backyard. There was a spotlight and the children's laughter. I could almost make out my sister's hair, and my brother's laugh, and, well, there I was with my black mittens. I stood in the road and watched the children.

Tonight I'll make my wife a cup of hot chocolate. We received a call from a friend in Canada to say that her father died last week and his body is in the vault waiting for burial this spring when the ground thaws.

Even though the snow geese billowed out before me in glory, even though the children laughed as they cut across the smooth ice, it is still cold and I long for spring.

I liked being a seventeen-year-old high school boy waving to my grandmother as she looked up from her newspaper in the warm, April air.

Though I yearn for your kingdom, though I long for your embrace, I pray to you my God that you come to me today as I sit and wrap my shawl around my shoulders.

Epilogue

"Finally, brothers, whatever is true, whatever is noble, whatever is right, whatever is pure, whatever is lovely, whatever is admirable—if anything is excellent or praiseworthy—think about such things. Whatever you have learned or received or heard from me, or seen in me—put it into practice. And the God of peace will be with you."

PHILIPPIANS 4:8-9

Christopher de Vinck is available for
speaking engagements. Contact him directly at
devinck@sprynet.com